An expository study
of Romans

Warren W. Wiersbe

This book is designed for your personal reading pleasure and profit. It is also designed
for group study. A leader's guide with helps
and hints for teachers and visual aids (Victor
Multi-use Transparency Masters) is available
from your local bookstore or from the pub-
lisher at $2.25.

VICTOR BOOKS
a division of SP Publications, Inc., Wheaton, Illinois
Offices also in Fullerton, California • Whitby, Ontario, Canada • London, England

Bible quotations are from the King James Version unless otherwise noted. Other quotations are from the *New American Standard Bible* (NASB), © The Lockman Foundation, La Habra, Calif., 1960, 1962, 1963, 1968, 1971, 1972, 1973; *The New International Version: New Testament* (NIV), © 1973, The New York Bible Society; *The New Testament in the Language of the People* by Charles B. Williams (WMS), © 1966, Moody Press, Chicago, Ill. All quotations used by permission.

Library of Congress Catalog Card Number:
ISBN: 0-88207-729-5

VICTOR BOOKS
A Division of SP Publications, Inc.,
P. O. Box 1825 • Wheaton, Illinois 60187

Table of Contents

Dedicated to
DAVID
CAROLYN
BOB and
JUDY
with their father's
love and appreciation

Preface

If you are tired of all the wrong things in your life, in the lives of others, and in this world, then Paul's Epistle to the Romans is the book for you.

The theme of Romans is "the righteousness of God." In this letter, Paul tells how to *Be Right*—with God, ourselves, and others. Paul also explains how one day God will make creation right, and even solve "the Jewish problem" and bring peace on earth.

The Epistle to the Romans was not written for woolgatherers or religious sightseers. You will have to *think* as you study this letter, but the rewards will be worth the efforts. If you understand Romans, you will have the key to understanding the rest of the Bible. Better still, you will have the secret of successful Christian living.

Be Right is not a detailed explanation of Romans. It is an expository survey that helps you understand the main message of the letter and how it applies to your life today. After you have mastered this book, you can turn to the more detailed commentaries and, I trust, be better prepared to benefit from them.

WARREN W. WIERSBE
Moody Church, Chicago

Romans 1:1-17

Paul, a servant of Jesus Christ, called to be an apostle, separated unto the gospel of God, [2] (Which He had promised afore by His prophets in the holy Scriptures,) [3] Concerning His Son Jesus Christ our Lord, which was made of the seed of David according to the flesh; [4] And declared to be the Son of God with power, according to the Spirit of Holiness, by the resurrection from the dead: [5] By whom we have received grace and apostleship, for obedience to the faith among all nations, for His name: [6] Among whom are ye also called of Jesus Christ: [7] To all that be in Rome, beloved of God, called to be saints: Grace to you and peace from God our Father, and the Lord Jesus Christ. [8] First, I thank my God through Jesus Christ for you all, that your faith is spoken of throughout the whole world. [9] For God is my witness, whom I serve with my spirit in the Gospel of His Son, that without ceasing I make mention of you always in my prayers; [10] Making request, if by any means now at length I might have a prosperous journey by the will of God to come unto you. [11] For I long to see you, that I may impart unto you some spiritual gift, to the end ye may be established; [12] That is, that I may be comforted together with you by the mutual faith both of you and me. [13] Now I would not have you ignorant, brethren, that oftentimes I purposed to come unto you, (but was let hitherto,) that I might have some fruit among you also, even as among other Gentiles. [14] I am debtor both to the Greeks, and to the Barbarians; both to the wise, and to the unwise. [15] So, as much as in me is, I am ready to preach the Gospel to you that are at Rome also. [16] For I am not ashamed of the Gospel of Christ: for it is the power of God unto salvation to every one that believeth; to the Jew first, and also to the Greek. [17] For therein is the righteousness of God revealed from faith to faith: as it is written, "The just shall live by faith."

1

Ready for Rome

On May 24, 1738, a discouraged missionary went "very unwillingly" to a religious meeting in London. There a miracle took place. "About a quarter before nine," he wrote in his journal, "I felt my heart strangely warmed. I felt I did trust in Christ, Christ alone, for salvation; and an assurance was given me that He had taken away my sins, even mine, and saved me from the law of sin and death."

That missionary was John Wesley. The message he heard that evening was the preface to Martin Luther's commentary on Romans. Just a few months before, Wesley wrote in his journal: "I went to America to convert the Indians; but Oh! who shall convert me?" That evening in Aldersgate Street, his question was answered. And the result was the great Wesleyan Revival that swept England and transformed the nation.

Paul's Epistle to the Romans is still transforming people's lives, just the way it transformed Martin Luther and John Wesley. The one Scripture above all others that brought Luther out of mere religion into the joy of salvation by grace, through faith, was Romans 1:17: "The just shall live by faith." The Protestant Reformation and the Wesleyan Revival were both the fruit of this wonderful letter written by Paul from Corinth about the year A.D. 56. The letter was carried to the Christians at Rome by one of the deaconesses of the church at Cenchrea, Sister Phebe (Rom. 16:1).

Imagine! You and I can read and study the same inspired letter that brought life and power to Luther and Wesley! And the same Holy Spirit who taught them can teach us! You and I can experience revival in our hearts, homes, and churches if the message of this letter grips us as it has gripped men of faith in centuries past.

In the opening verses of the letter, Paul introduces himself to the believers in Rome. Some of them must have known him personally, since he greets them in the final chapter; but many of them he had never met. So, in these first 17 verses, Paul seeks to link himself to his Roman readers in three ways.

1. He Presents His Credentials (1:1-7)

In ancient days, the writer of a letter always opened with his name. But there would be many men named Paul in that day, so the writer must further identify himself and convince the readers that he has a right to send the letter. What are Paul's credentials?

a. *He is a servant of Jesus Christ* (1:1a)—The word Paul uses for *servant* would be meaningful to the Romans, because it is the word *slave*. There were an estimated six million slaves in the Roman Empire; and a slave was looked upon as a piece of property, not a person. In loving devotion, Paul had enslaved himself to Christ, to be His servant and obey His will.

b. *He is an apostle* (1:1b)—This word means "one who is sent by authority with a commission." It was applied in that day to the representatives of the emperor or the emissaries of a king. One of the requirements for an apostle was the experience of seeing the risen Christ (1 Cor. 9:1-2). Paul saw Christ when he was on the road to Damascus (Acts 9:1-9), and it was then that Christ called him to be His apostle to the Gentiles. Paul received from Christ divine revelations that he was to share with the churches.

c. *He is a preacher of the Gospel* (1:1c-4)— When he was a Jewish rabbi, Paul was separated as a Pharisee to the laws and traditions of the Jews. But when he yielded to Christ, he was separated to the Gospel and its ministry. *Gospel* means "the Good News." It is the message that Christ died for our sins, was buried, and rose again, and now is able to save all who trust Him (1 Cor. 15:1-4). It is "the Gospel of God" (Rom. 1:1) because it originates with God; it was not invented by man. It is "the Gospel of Christ" (1:16) because it centers in Christ, the Saviour. Paul also calls it "the Gospel of His Son" (1:9), which indicates that *Jesus Christ is God!* In Romans 16:25-26, Paul calls it "my Gospel." By this he means the special emphasis he gave in his ministry to the doctrine of the Church and the place of the Gentiles in the plan of God.

The Gospel is not a new message; it was promised in the Old Testament, beginning in Genesis 3:15. The Prophet Isaiah certainly preached the Gospel in passages such as 1:18, and chapters 53 and 55. The salvation we enjoy today was promised by the prophets, though they did not fully understand all that they were preaching and writing (1 Peter 1:10-12).

Jesus Christ is the center of the Gospel message. Paul identifies Him as a man, a Jew, and the Son of God. He was born of a virgin (Isa. 7:14; Matt. 1:18-25) into the family of David, which gave Him the right to David's throne. He died for the sins of the world, and then was raised from the dead. It is this miraculous event of substitutionary death and victorious resurrection that constitutes the Gospel; and it was this Gospel that Paul preached.

d. *He is a missionary to the Gentiles* (1:5-7)— *Missionary* is the Latin form of "apostle—one who is sent." There were probably several assemblies of believers in Rome and not just one church, since in Romans 16 Paul greets a number of "home church" groups (16:5, 10, 11, 14). We do not know for certain how these churches began, but it is likely that believers from Rome who were at Pentecost established the assemblies on their return to Rome (Acts 2:10). There were both Jews and Gentiles in these fellowships, because Paul addresses both in this letter. (Jews 2:17-29; 4:1; 7:1. Gentiles: 1:13, 11:13-24; 15:15-21.) The churches in Rome were not founded by Peter or any other apostle. If they had been, Paul would not have planned to visit Rome, because his policy was to minister only where no other apostle had gone (Rom. 15:20-21).

Note the repetition of the word *called*: Paul was called to be an apostle; the believers were the called of Jesus Christ; and they were also called saints. (Not "to be" saints; they already were saints! A saint is a set-apart one, and the person who trusts Jesus Christ is set apart and is a saint.) Salvation is not something that we do for God; it is God who calls us in His grace (2 Thes. 2:13-14). When you trust Christ, you are saved by His grace and you experience His peace.

Paul's special commission was to take the Gospel to the Gentiles (the word *nations* means Gentiles), and this is why he was planning to go to Rome, the very capital of the empire. He was a preacher of the Gospel, and the Gospel was for all nations. In fact, Paul was anxious to go to Spain with the message of Christ (Rom. 15:28).

Having presented his credentials, Paul proceeds to forge a second link between himself and the believers in Rome.

2. He Expresses His Concern (1:8-15)

We can well understand Paul's concern for the churches that he founded, but why would he be concerned about the believers at Rome? He was unknown to many of them, yet he wanted to assure them that he was deeply concerned about their welfare. Note the evidences of Paul's concern.

a. *He was thankful for them* (1:8)—"The whole world"—meaning the whole Roman Empire—knew of the faith of the Christians at Rome. Travel was relatively common in that day and "all roads led to Rome." It is no wonder that the testimony of the church spread abroad, and this growing witness made Paul's ministry easier as he went from place to place, and was able to point to this testimony going out from the heart of the Roman Empire.

b. *He prayed for them* (1:9-10)—They did not know of Paul's prayer support, but the Lord knew about it and honored it. (I wonder how many of us know the people who are praying for us?) One of the burdens of Paul's prayer was that God would permit him to visit Rome and minister to the churches there. He would have visited them sooner, but his missionary work had kept him busy (Rom. 15:15-33). He was about to leave Corinth for Jerusalem to deliver the special offering received from the Gentile churches for the poor Jewish saints. He hoped he would be able to travel from Jerusalem to Rome, and then on to Spain; and he was hoping for a prosperous journey.

Actually, Paul had a very perilous journey; and he arrived in Rome a prisoner as well as a preacher. In Jerusalem he was arrested in the temple, falsely accused by the Jewish authorities and eventually sent to Rome as the Emperor's prisoner to be tried before Caesar. When Paul wrote this letter, he had no idea that he would go through imprisonment and even shipwreck before arriving in Rome! At the close of the letter (15:30-33), he asked the believers in Rome to pray for him as he contemplated this trip; and it is a good thing that they did pray!

c. *He loved them* (1:11-12)—"I long to see you!" This is the pastor's heart in Paul the great missionary. Some of the saints in Rome were very dear to Paul, such as Priscilla and Aquila (16:3-4), who risked their lives for him; "the beloved Persis" (16:12); and others who had labored and suffered with Paul. But he also loved the believers that he did not know, and he longed to be able to share some spiritual gift with them. He was looking forward to a time of mutual blessing in the love of Christ.

d. *He was in debt to them* (1:13-14)—As the apostle to the Gentiles, Paul had an obligation to minister in Rome. He would have fulfilled that obligation sooner, but his other labors had hindered him. Sometimes Paul was hindered because of the work of Satan (1 Thes. 2:17-20); but in this case he was hindered because of the work of the Lord.

There was so much to do in Asia Minor and Greece that he could not immediately spare time for Rome. But Paul had to pay his debt; he was under orders from the Lord.

The Greeks considered every non-Greek a barbarian. Steeped in centuries of philosophy, the Greeks saw themselves as wise and everyone else as foolish. But Paul felt an obligation to *all* men, just as we need to feel a burden for the whole world. Paul could not be free from his debt until he had told as many people as possible the Good News of salvation in Christ.

e. *He was eager to visit them* (1:15)—Two different Greek words are translated "ready" in the King James Version. One means "prepared," as in Acts 21:13. "I am ready . . . to die at Jerusalem for the name of the Lord Jesus." The other one, used in Romans 1:15, means "eager, with a ready mind." Paul was not eager to die, although he was prepared to die. But he was eager to visit Rome that he might minister to the believers there. It was not the eagerness of a sightseer, but the eagerness of a soul-winner.

After reading these five evidences of Paul's concern for the Christians at Rome, these saints could not but give thanks to God for the Apostle Paul and his burden to come and minister to them. Actually, the Epistle to the Romans in which Paul explained the Gospel he preached, was his letter of introduction that prepared the believers for his visit. No doubt the false teachers had already gotten to Rome and were seeking to poison the Christians against Paul (see Rom. 3:8). Some would accuse him of being anti-Law; others would say he was a traitor to the Jewish nation. Still others would twist his teaching about grace and try to prove that he taught loose living. No wonder Paul was eager to get to Rome! He wanted to share with them the fulness of the Gospel of Christ.

But would the Gospel of Christ work in the great city of Rome as it had in other places? Would Paul succeed there, or would he fail? The apostle no doubt felt these objections and raised these questions in his own mind, which is why he forged a third link between himself and his readers.

3. He Affirms His Confidence (1:16-17)

What a testimony: "I am debtor! I am eager! I am not ashamed!" Why would Paul even be tempted to be ashamed of the Gospel as he contemplated his trip to Rome? For one thing, the Gospel was identified with a poor Jewish carpenter who was crucified. The Romans had no special appreciation for the Jews, and crucifixion was the lowest form of execution given a criminal. Why put your faith in a Jew who was crucified?

Rome was a proud city, and the Gospel came from Jerusalem, the capital city of one of the little nations that Rome had conquered. The Christians in that day were not among the elite of society; they were common people and even slaves. Rome had known many great philosophers and philosophies; why pay any attention to a fable about a Jew who arose from the dead? (1 Cor. 1:18-25) Christians looked upon each other as brothers and sisters, all one in Christ, which went against the grain of Roman pride and dignity. To think of a little Jewish tentmaker, going to Rome to preach such a message, is almost humorous.

But Paul was not ashamed of the Gospel. He had confidence in his message, and he gave us several reasons that explain why he was not ashamed.

a. *The origin of the Gospel*: it is the Gospel of Christ (1:16a)—Any message that was handed down from Caesar would immediately get the attention of the Romans. But the message of the Gospel is from and about the very Son of God! In his opening sentence, Paul called this message "the Gospel of God" (1:1). How could Paul be ashamed of such a message, when it came from God and centered in His Son, Jesus Christ?

During my years in high school, I was chosen to be an office monitor. The other hall monitors sat at various stations around the buildings, but I was privileged to sit right outside the door of the main high school office. I was entrusted with important messages that I had to deliver to different teachers and staff members, and on occasion even to other schools. Believe me, it was fun to walk into a classroom and even interrupt a lesson! No teacher ever scolded me, because all of them knew I carried messages from the principal. I never had to be afraid or ashamed, because I knew where my messages came from.

b. *The operation of the Gospel*: it is the power of God (1:16b)—Why be ashamed of power? Power is the one thing that Rome boasted of the most. Greece might have its philosophy, but Rome had its power. The fear of Rome hovered over the empire like a cloud. Were they not the conquerors? Were not the Roman legions stationed all over the known world? But with all of her military power, Rome was still a weak nation. The philosopher Seneca called the city of Rome "a cesspool of iniquity"; and the writer Juvenal called it a "filthy sewer into which the dregs of the empire flood."

No wonder Paul was not ashamed: he was taking to sinful Rome the one message that had the power to change men's lives! He had seen the Gospel work in other wicked cities such as Corinth and Ephesus; and he was confident that it would work in Rome. It had transformed his own life, and he knew it could transform the lives of others. There was a third reason why Paul was not ashamed.

c. *The outcome of the Gospel*: it is the power of God unto salvation (1:16c)—That word "salvation" carried tremendous meaning in Paul's day. Its basic meaning is "deliverance," and it was applied to personal and national deliverance. The emperor was looked upon as a savior, as was the physician who healed you of illness. The Gospel delivers sinners from the penalty and power of sin. "Salvation" is a major theme in this letter; salvation is the great need of the human race. (See Rom. 10:1, 9-10.) If men and women are to be saved, it must be through faith in Jesus Christ as proclaimed in the Gospel.

d. *The outreach of the Gospel:* "to everyone that believeth" (1:16d)—This was not an exclusive message for either the Jew or the Gentile; it was for all men, *because all men need to be saved.* "Go ye into all the world and preach the Gospel," was Christ's commission (Mark 16:15). "To the Jew first" does not suggest that the Jew is better than the Gentile; for there is "no difference" in condemnation or in salvation (Rom. 2:6-11; 10:9-13). The Gospel came "to the Jew first" in the ministry of Jesus Christ (Matt. 10:5-7) and the apostles (Acts 3:26). How marvelous it is to have a message of power that can be taken to *all* people!

God does not ask men to *behave,* but to *believe.* It is faith in Christ that saves the sinner. Eternal life in Christ is one gift that is suitable for all people, no matter what their need may be or what their station in life.

Romans 1:17 is the key verse of the letter. In it Paul announces the theme: "the righteousness of God." The word "righteousness" is used in one way or another over sixty times in this letter (righteous, just, and justified). God's righteousness is revealed in the Gospel; for in the death of Christ, God revealed His righteousness by punishing sin; and in the resurrection of Christ, He revealed His righteousness by making salvation available to the believing sinner. The problem "How can a holy God ever forgive sinners and still be holy?" is answered in the Gospel. Through the death and resurrection of Christ, God is seen to be "both just and justifier" (Rom. 3:26).

The Gospel reveals a righteousness that is *by faith*. In the Old Testament, righteousness was *by* works, but sinners soon discovered they could not obey God's Law and meet His righteous demands. Here Paul refers to Habakkuk 2:4: "The just shall live by his faith." This verse is quoted three times in the New Testament: Romans 1:17; Galatians 3:11; and Hebrews 10:38. Romans explains "the just"; Galatians explains "shall live"; and Hebrews explains "by faith." There are more than 60 references to faith or unbelief in Romans, because the only way a sinner can become just before God is "by faith."

If at this point in his letter Paul had inserted an outline of his letter, it would have looked something like this:

Theme: The righteousness of God
Text: "The just shall live by faith"
Introduction—1:1-17

When you study Romans, you walk into a courtroom. First, Paul called Jews and Gentiles to the stand and found both guilty before God. Then he explained God's marvelous way of salvation—justification by faith. At this point, he answered his accusers and defended God's salvation. "This plan of salvation will encourage people to sin!" they cry. "It is against the very Law of God!" But Paul refuted them, and in so doing explained how the Christian can experience victory, liberty, and security.

Chapters 9—11 are not a parenthesis or a detour. There were Jewish believers in the Roman assemblies and they would naturally ask, "What about Israel? How does God's righteousness relate to them in this new age of the Church?" In these three chapters, Paul gave a complete history of Israel, past, present, and future.

Then he concluded with the practical outworking of God's righteousness in the life of the believer. This begins with dedication to God (12:1-2), continues with ministry in the church (12:3-21), and then obedience to the government (13:1-14). He also told Jews and Gentiles, strong and weak, how to live together in harmony and joy. In the closing section (15:14—16:27), Paul explained his plans and greeted his friends.

When you sum it all up, the Book of Romans is saying to us—*"Be right!"* Be right with God, with yourself, and with others! The righteousness of God received by faith makes it possible for us to live right lives. Rome needed this message, and we need it today: *Be right!*

18 For the wrath of God is revealed from heaven against all ungodliness and unrighteousness of men, who hold the truth in unrighteousness; [19] Because that which may be known of God is manifest in them; for God hath showed it unto them. [20] For the invisible things of Him from the creation of the world are clearly seen, being understood by the things that are made, even His eternal power and Godhead; so that they are without excuse.

(Romans 1:18-20)

26 For this cause God gave them up into vile affections: for even their women did change the natural use into that which is against nature: [27] And likewise also the men, leaving the natural use of the woman, burned in their lust one toward another; men with men working that which is unseemly, and received into themselves that recompence of their error which was meet. [28] And even as they did not like to retain God in their knowledge, God gave them over to a reprobate mind, to do those things which are not convenient.

(Romans 1:26-28)

Therefore thou art inexcusable, O man, whosoever thou art that judgest: for wherein thou judgest another, thou condemnest thyself; for thou that judgest doest the same things. [2] But we are sure that the judgment of God is according to truth against them which commit such things. [3] And thinkest thou this, O man, that judgest them which do such things, and doest the same, that thou shalt escape the judgment of God? [4] Or despisest thou the riches of His goodness and forbearance and longsuffering; not knowing that the goodness of God leadeth thee to repentance? [5] But after thy hardness and impenitent heart treasurest up unto thyself wrath against the day of wrath and revelation of the righteous judgment of God; [6] who will render to every man according to his deeds.

(Romans 2:1-6)

2

When God
Gives Up

"Hear ye! Hear ye! Court is now in session!" Paul
could have used those awesome words at this point
in his letter, because Romans 1:18 is the door that
leads us into God's courtroom. The theme of
Romans is the righteousness of God, but Paul had
to begin with the *un*righteousness of man. Until
man knows he is a sinner, he cannot appreciate the
gracious salvation God offers in Jesus Christ. Paul
followed the basic Bible pattern: first Law and
condemnation; then grace and salvation.

In this section, God makes three declarations
that together prove that all men are sinners and
need Jesus Christ.

1. The Gentile World is Guilty! (1:18-32)
The picture Paul paints here is an ugly one. I
confess that there are some neighborhoods in
Chicago that I dislike driving through, and I avoid

them if I can. My avoiding them does not change them or eliminate them. God's description of sinners is not a pretty one, but we cannot avoid it. This section does not teach evolution (that man started low and climbed high), but *devolution:* he started high and, because of sin, sank lower than the beasts. Four stages mark man's tragic devolution.

a. *Intelligence* (1:18-20)—Human history began with man knowing God. Human history is not the story of a beast that worshiped idols, and then evolved into a man worshiping one God. Human history is just the opposite: man began knowing God, but turned from the truth and rejected God. God revealed Himself to man through creation, the things that He made. From the world around him, man knew that there was a God who had the wisdom to plan and the power to create. Man realized, too, that this Creator was eternal . . . "His eternal power and Godhead" (v. 20), since God could not be created if He is the Creator. These facts about God are not hidden in creation; they are "clearly seen" (v. 20). "The heavens declare the glory of God, and the firmament showeth His handiwork" (Ps. 19:1).

The word translated "hold" in verse 18 can also be translated "hold down, suppress." Men knew the truth about God, but they did not allow this truth to work in their lives. They suppressed it in order that they might live their own lives and not be convicted by God's truth. The result, of course, was refusing the truth (1:21-22), and then turning the truth into a lie (1:25). Finally, man so abandoned the truth that he became like a beast in his thinking and in his living.

b. *Ignorance* (1:21-23)—Man knew God; this is

clear. But man did not *want* to know God or honor Him as God. Instead of being thankful for all that God had given him, man refused to thank God or give Him the glory He deserves. Man was willing to use God's gifts, but he was not willing to worship and praise God for His gifts. The result was an empty mind and a darkened heart. Man the worshiper became man the philosopher, but his empty wisdom only revealed his foolishness. Paul summarized all of Greek history in one dramatic statement: "the times of this ignorance . . ." (Acts 17:30). First Corinthians 1:18-31 is worth reading at this point.

Having held down God's truth and refusing to acknowledge God's glory, man was left without a god; and man is so constituted that he must worship something. If he will not worship the true God, he will worship a false god, *even if he has to manufacture it himself!* This fact about man accounts for his propensity to idolatry. Man exchanged the glory of the true God for substitute gods that he himself made. He exchanged glory for shame, incorruption for corruption, truth for lies.

Note that first on the list of false gods is *man*. This fulfilled Satan's purpose when he told Eve, "Ye shall be as God!" (Gen. 3:5, NASB) "Glory to man in the highest!" Satan encouraged man to say. Instead of man being made in God's image, man made gods in his own image—and then descended so low as to worship birds, beasts, and bugs!

c. *Indulgence* (1:24-27)—From idolatry to immorality is just one short step. If man is his own god, then he can do whatever he pleases and fulfill his desires without fear of judgment. We reach the climax of man's battle with God's truth when man exchanges the truth of God for "the lie" and abandons truth completely. "The lie" is that man is his own god, and he should worship and serve himself and not the Creator. It was "the lie" Satan used in the Garden to lead Eve into sin: "Ye shall be as God!" Satan has always wanted the worship that belongs only to God (Matt. 4:8-10); and in idolatry, he receives that worship (1 Cor. 10:19-21).

The result of this self-deification was self-indulgence; and here Paul mentions a vile sin that was rampant in that day and has become increasingly prevalent in our own day: homosexuality. This sin is repeatedly condemned in Scripture (Gen. 12:20ff; 1 Cor. 6:9-10; Jude 7). Paul characterizes it as "vile" and "unnatural," as well as "against nature." Not only were the men guilty, but "even the women."

Because of their sin "God gave them up" (1:24, 26) which means that He permitted them to go on in their sins and reap the sad consequences. They received "in their own persons the due penalty of their error" (1:27, NASB). This is the meaning of Romans 1:18, "The wrath of God is being revealed from heaven . . ." (literal translation). God revealed His wrath, not by sending fire from heaven, but by abandoning sinful men to their lustful ways. But there was one more stage.

d. *Impenitence* (1:28-32)—When man began to feel the tragic consequences of his sins, you would think he would repent and seek God; but just the opposite was true. Because he was abandoned by God, he could only become worse. Man did not even want to retain God in his knowledge! So, "God gave them over . . ." this time to a "depraved mind" (1:28, NASB), which means a mind that cannot form right judgments. They now abandoned themselves to sin. Paul names 24 specific sins, all of which are with us today. (For other lists, see Mark 7:20-23, Gal. 5:19-21, 1 Tim. 1:9-10, and 2 Tim. 3:2-5.)

But the worst is yet to come. Men not only committed these sins in open defiance of God, but encouraged others and applauded them when they sinned. How far man fell! He began glorifying God but ended exchanging that glory for idols. He began knowing God but ended refusing to keep the knowledge of God in his mind and heart. He began as the highest of God's creatures, made in the image of God but he ended lower than the beasts and insects, because he worshiped them as his gods. The verdict? "They are without excuse!" (1:20)

This portion of Scripture gives ample proof that the heathen are lost. Dan Crawford, British missionary to Africa, said: "The heathen are sinning against a flood of light." There is a desperate need for us to carry the Gospel to all men, for this is the only way they can be saved.

2. The Jewish World Is Guilty! (2:1—3:8)

Bible scholars do not agree on whom Paul was addressing in Romans 2:1-16. Some think he was dealing with the moral pagan who did not commit the sins named in Romans 1:18-32, but who sought to live a moral life. But it seems to me that Paul was addressing his Jewish readers in this section. To begin with, his discussion of the Law in 2:12-16 would have been more meaningful to a Jew than to a Gentile. And in 2:17, he openly addressed his reader as "a Jew." This would be a strange form of address if in the first half of the chapter he were addressing Gentiles.

It would not be an easy task to find the Jews guilty, since disobedience to God was one sin they did not want to confess. The Old Testament prophets were persecuted for indicting Israel for her sins, and Jesus was crucified for the same reason. Paul summoned four witnesses to prove the guilt of the Jewish nation.

a. *The Gentiles* (2:1-3)—Certainly the Jews would applaud Paul's condemnation of the Gentiles in Romans 1:18-32. In fact, Jewish national and religious pride encouraged them to despise the "Gentile dogs" and have nothing to do with them. Paul used this judgmental attitude to prove the guilt of the Jews; *for the very things they condemned in the Gentiles, they themselves were practicing!* They thought that they were free from judgment because they were God's chosen people. But Paul affirms that God's election of the Jews made their responsibility and accountability even greater.

God's judgment is according to truth. He does not have one standard for the Jews and another for the Gentiles. One who reads the list of sins in Romans 1:29-32 cannot escape the fact that each person is guilty of at least one of them. There are "sins of the flesh and of the spirit" (2 Cor. 7:1); there are "prodigal sons" and "elder brothers" (Luke 15:11-32). In condemning the Gentiles for their sins, the Jews were really condemning themselves. As the old saying puts it, "When you point your finger at somebody else, the other three are pointing at you."

b. *God's blessing* (2:4-11)—Instead of giving the Jews special treatment from God, the blessings they received from Him gave them greater responsibility to obey Him and glorify Him. In His goodness, God had given Israel great material and spiritual riches: a wonderful land, a righteous law, a temple and priesthood, God's providential care, and many more blessings. God had patiently endured Israel's many sins and rebellions, and had even sent them His Son to be their Messiah. Even after Israel crucified Christ, God gave the nation nearly forty more years of grace and withheld His judgment. It is not the *judgment* of God that leads men to repentance, but the *goodness* of God; but Israel did not repent.

In Romans 2:6-11, Paul was not teaching salvation by character or good deeds. He was explaining another basic principle of God's judgment: God judges according to deeds, just as He judges according to truth. Paul was dealing here with the consistent actions of a person's life, the total impact of his character and conduct. For example, David committed some terrible sins; but the total emphasis of his life was obedience to God. Judas confessed his sin and supplied the money for buying a cemetery for strangers; yet the total emphasis of his life was disobedience and unbelief.

True saving faith results in obedience and godly living, even though there may be occasional falls. When God measured the deeds of the Jews, He found them to be as wicked as those of the Gentiles. The fact that the Jews occasionally celebrated a feast or even regularly honored the Sabbath Day did not change the fact that their consistent daily life was one of disobedience to God. God's blessings did not lead them to repentance.

c. *God's Law* (2:12-24)—Paul's statement in verse 11, "For there is no respect of persons with God" would shock the Jew, for he considered himself deserving of special treatment because he was

chosen by God. But Paul explained that the Jewish
Law only made the guilt of Israel that much
greater! God did not give the Law to the Gentiles,
so they would not be judged by the Law. Actually,
the Gentiles had "the work of the Law written in
their hearts" (Rom. 2:15). Wherever you go, you
find people with an inner sense of right and wrong;
and this inner judge, the Bible calls "conscience."
You find among all cultures a sense of sin, a fear of
judgment, and an attempt to atone for sins and
appease whatever gods are feared.

The Jew boasted in the Law. He was different
from his pagan neighbors who worshiped idols!
But Paul made it clear that it was not the *posses-
sion* of the Law that counted, but the *practice* of
the Law. The Jews looked upon the Gentiles as
blind, in the dark, foolish, immature, and ignorant!
But if God found the "deprived" Gentiles guilty,
how much more guilty were the "privileged" Jews!
God not only judges according to truth (2:2), and
according to men's deeds (2:6); but He also judges
"the secrets of men" (2:16). He sees what is in the
heart!

The Jewish people had a religion of outward
action, not inward attitude. They may have been
moral on the outside, but what about the heart?
Our Lord's indictment of the Pharisees in Matthew
23 illustrates the principle perfectly. God not only
sees the deeds but He also sees the "thoughts and
intents of the heart" (Heb. 4:12). It is possible
for a Jew to be guilty of theft, adultery, and idolatry (vv. 21-22) even if no one saw him commit
these sins outwardly. In the Sermon on the Mount
we are told that such sins can be committed in
the heart.

Instead of glorifying God among the Gentiles,

the Jews were dishonoring God; and Paul quoted Isaiah 52:5 to prove his point. The pagan Gentiles had daily contact with the Jews in business and other activities, and they were not fooled by the Jews' devotion to the Law. The very Law that the Jews claimed to obey only indicted them!

d. *Circumcision* (2:25-29)—This was the great mark of the covenant, and it had its beginning with Abraham, the father of the Jewish nation (Gen. 17). To the Jews, the Gentiles were "uncircumcised dogs." The tragedy is that the Jews depended on this physical mark instead of the spiritual reality it represented (Deut. 10:16; Jer. 9:26; Ezek. 44:9). A true Jew is one who has had an *inward* spiritual experience in the heart, and not merely an outward physical operation. People today make this same mistake with reference to baptism or the Lord's Supper, or even church membership.

God judges according to "the secrets of the heart" (Rom. 2:16), so that He is not impressed with mere outward formalities. An obedient Gentile with no circumcision would be more acceptable than a disobedient Jew with circumcision. In fact, a disobedient Jew turns his circumcision into *un*circumcision in God's sight, for God looks at the heart. The Jews praised each other for their obedience to the Law, but the important thing is the "praise of God" and not the praise of men (v. 29). When you recall that the name "Jew" comes from "Judah" which means "praise," this statement takes on new meaning (Gen. 29:35; 49:8).

All of Paul's four witnesses agreed: the Jews were guilty before God. In Romans 3:1-8, Paul summed up the argument and refuted those Jews who tried to debate with him. They raised three

questions. (1) "What advantage is it to be a Jew?"
Reply: Every advantage, especially possessing the
Word of God. (2) "Will Jewish unbelief cancel
God's faithfulness?" Reply: Absolutely not—it
establishes it. (3) "If our sin commends His
righteousness, how can He judge us?" Reply: We
do not do evil that good may come of it. God judges
the world righteously.

3. The Whole World is Guilty! (3:9-20)

The third declaration was obvious, for Paul had
already proved (charged) both Jews and Gentiles
to be guilty before God. Next he declared that all
men were sinners, and proved it with several quotations from the Old Testament. Note the repetition
of the words "none" and "all," which in themselves
assert the universality of human guilt.

His first quotation was from Psalm 14:1-3. This
psalm begins with, "The fool hath said in his heart,
'There is no God.'" The words "there is" are in
italics, meaning they were added by the transla-
tors; so you can read the sentence, "The fool hath
said in his heart, 'No, God!'" This parallels the
description of man's devolution given in Romans
1:18-32, for it all started with man saying "No!"
to God.

These verses indicate that the whole of man's
inner being is controlled by sin: his *mind* ("none
that understandeth"), his *heart* ("none that seeketh
after God"), and his *will* ("none that doeth good").
Measured by God's perfect righteousness, no human
being is sinless. No sinner seeks after God. Therefore, God must seek the sinner (Gen. 3:8-10; Luke
19:10). Man has gone astray, and has become
unprofitable both to himself and to God. Our Lord's
parables in Luke 15 illustrate this perfectly.

In 13-18, Paul gave us an X-ray study of the lost sinner, from head to foot. His quotations are as follows: 13a—Psalm 5:9; 13b—Psalm 140:3; 14—Psalm 10:7; 15-17—Isaiah 59:7-8; 18—Psalm 36:1. These verses need to be read in their contexts for the full impact.

Verses 13 and 14 emphasize human speech—the throat, tongue, lips, and mouth. The connection between words and character is seen in Matthew 12:34: "For out of the abundance of the heart the mouth speaketh." The sinner is spiritually dead by nature (Eph. 2:1-3), therefore only death can come out of his mouth. The condemned mouth can become a converted mouth and acknowledge that "Jesus Christ is Lord" (Rom. 10:9-10). "For by thy words thou shalt be justified, and by thy words thou shalt be condemned" (Matt. 12:37).

In verses 15 and 16, Paul pictured the sinner's feet. Just as his words are deceitful, so his ways are destructive. The Christian's feet are shod with the Gospel of peace (Eph. 6:15); but the lost sinner brings death, destruction, and misery wherever he goes. These tragedies may not occur immediately, but they will come inevitably. The lost sinner is on the broad road that leads to destruction (Matt. 7:13-14); he needs to repent, trust Jesus Christ, and get on the narrow road that leads to life.

Verse 17 deals with the sinner's mind: he does not know the way of God's peace. This is what caused Jesus to weep over Jerusalem (Luke 19:41-44). The sinner does not want to know God's truth (Rom. 1:21, 25, 28); he prefers to believe Satan's lie. God's way of peace is through Jesus Christ: "Therefore being justified by faith, we have peace with God through our Lord Jesus Christ" (Rom. 5:1).

In verse 18, which cites Psalm 36:1, the sinner's arrogant pride is described: "There is no fear of God before their eyes." The entire Psalm should be read to get the full picture. The ignorance mentioned in Romans 3:17 is caused by the pride of verse 18; for it is "the fear of the Lord" that is the beginning of knowledge (Prov. 1:7).

These quotations from God's Law, the Old Testament Scriptures, lead to one conclusion: *the whole world is guilty before God!* There may be those who want to argue, but every mouth is stopped. There is no debate or defense. The whole world is guilty, Jews and Gentiles. The Jews stand condemned by the Law of which they boast, and the Gentiles stand condemned on the basis of creation and conscience.

The word "therefore" in verse 20 carries the meaning of "because," and gives the reason why the whole world is guilty. No flesh can obey God's Law and be justified (declared righteous) in His sight. It is true that "the doers of the law shall be justified" (Rom. 2:13), but *nobody can do what the Law demands!* This inability is one way that men know they are sinners. When they try to obey the Law, they fail miserably and need to cry out for God's mercy. Neither Jew nor Gentile can obey God's Law; therefore God must save sinners by some other means. The explanation of that means by which man can be saved occupied Paul for the rest of his letter.

The best way to close this section would be to ask a simple question: Has your mouth ever been stopped? Are you boasting of your own self-righteousness and defending yourself before God? If so, then perhaps you have never been saved by God's grace. It is only when we stand silent before

Him as sinners that He can save us. As long as we defend ourselves and commend ourselves, we cannot be saved by God's grace. The whole world is guilty before God—and that includes you and me!

21 But now the righteousness of God without the law is manifested, being witnessed by the law and the prophets: ²² Even the righteousness of God which is by faith of Jesus Christ unto all and upon all them that believe: for there is no difference: ²³ For all have sinned, and come short of the glory of God; ²⁴ Being justified freely by His grace through the redemption that is in Christ Jesus: ²⁵ Whom God hath set forth to be a propitiation through faith in His blood, to declare His righteousness for the remission of sins that are past, through the forbearance of God; ²⁶ To declare, I say, at this time His righteousness: that He might be just, and the justifier of him who believeth in Jesus. ²⁷ Where is boasting then? It is excluded. By what law? of works? Nay: but by the law of faith.

(Romans 3:21-27)

13 For the promise, that he should be the heir of the world, was not to Abraham, or to his seed, through the law, but through the righteousness of faith. ¹⁴ For if they which are of the law be heirs, faith is made void, and the promise made of none effect: ¹⁵ Because the law worketh wrath: for where no law is, there is no transgression. ¹⁶ Therefore it is of faith, that it might be by grace; to the end the promise might be sure to all the seed; not to that only which is of the law, but to that also which is of the faith of Abraham: who is the father of us all, ¹⁷ (As it is written, I have made thee a father of many nations,) before Him whom he believed, even God, who quickeneth the dead, and calleth those things which be not as though they were.

(Romans 4:13-17)

3

Father Abraham

Paul's theme in the second section of his letter was *Salvation—Righteousness Declared*. He had proved that all men are sinners; next he was to explain how sinners can be saved. The theological term for this salvation is *justification by faith*. Justification is the act of God whereby He declares the believing sinner righteous in Christ on the basis of the finished work of Christ on the cross. Each part of this definition is important, so we must consider it carefully.

To begin with, justification is an *act*, not a process. There are no degrees of justification; each believer has the same right standing before God. Also, justification is something *God* does, not man. No sinner can justify himself before God. Most important, justification does not mean that God *makes* us righteous, but that He *declares* us righteous. Justification is a legal matter. God puts the righteousness of Christ on our record in the place of our own sinfulness. And nobody can change this record.

Do not confuse justification and sanctification. Sanctification is the process whereby God makes the believer more and more like Christ. Sanctification may change from day to day. Justification never changes. When the sinner trusts Christ, God declares him righteous, and that declaration will never be repealed. God looks upon us and deals with us as though we had never sinned at all!

But, how can a holy God declare sinners righteous? Is justification merely a "fictional idea" that has no real foundation? In this section of Romans, Paul answered these questions in two ways. First, he explained justification by faith (3:21-31); then he illustrated justification by faith from the life of Abraham (4:1-25).

1. Justification Explained (3:21-31)

"But now the righteousness of God . . . has been manifested." (Rom. 3:21, literal translation). God had revealed His righteousness in many ways before the full revelation of the Gospel: His Law, His judgments against sin, His appeals through the prophets, His blessing on the obedient. But in the Gospel, a new kind of righteousness has been revealed (Rom. 1:16-17); and the characteristics of this righteousness are spelled out in this section.

a. *Apart from the Law* (3:21)—Under the Old Testament Law, righteousness came by man *behaving;* but under the Gospel, righteousness comes by *believing.* The Law itself reveals the righteousness of God, because the Law is "holy and just and good" (Rom. 7:12). Furthermore, the Law bore witness to this Gospel righteousness even though it could not provide it. Beginning at Genesis 3:15, and continuing through the entire Old Testament, witness is given to salvation by faith in Christ.

The Old Testament sacrifices, the prophecies, the types, and the great "Gospel Scriptures" (such as Isa. 53) all bore witness to this truth. The Law could witness to God's righteousness, but it could not provide it for sinful man. Only Jesus Christ could do that. (See Gal. 2:21.)

b. *Through faith in Christ* (3:22a)—Faith is only as good as its object. All men trust something, if only themselves; but the Christian trusts Christ. Law righteousness is a reward for works. Gospel righteousness is a gift through faith. Many people say, "I trust in God!" But this is not what saves us. It is personal, individual faith in Jesus Christ that saves and justifies the lost sinner. Even the demons from hell believe in God and tremble, yet this does not save them (James 2:19).

c. *For all men* (3:22b-23)—God gave His Law to the Jews, not to the Gentiles; but the Good News of salvation through Christ is offered to all men. All men need to be saved. There is no difference between the Jew and the Gentile when it comes to condemnation. "All have sinned, and are coming short of the glory of God" (Rom. 3:23, literal translation). God declared all men guilty so that He might offer to all men His free gift of salvation.

d. *By grace* (3:24)—God has two kinds of attributes: *absolute* (what He is in Himself), and *relative* (how He relates to the world and men). One of His absolute attributes is love: "God is love" (1 John 4:8). When God relates that love to you and me, it becomes *grace* and *mercy*. God in His mercy does not give us what we do deserve, and God in grace gives us what we do not deserve. The Greek word translated "freely" is translated in John 15:25 as "without a cause." We are justified *without a cause!* There is no cause in us that would merit the salvation of God! It is all of grace!

e. *At great cost to God* (3:24b-25)—Salvation is free, but it is not cheap. Three words express the price God paid for our salvation: propitiation, redemption, and blood. In human terms, "propitiation" means appeasing someone who is angry, usually by a gift. But this is not what it means in the Bible. "Propitiation" means the satisfying of God's holy Law, the meeting of its just demands, so that God can freely forgive those who come to Christ. The word "blood" tells us what the price was. Jesus had to die on the cross in order to satisfy the Law and justify lost sinners.

The best illustration of this truth is the Jewish Day of Atonement described in Leviticus 16. Two goats were presented at the altar, and one of them was chosen for a sacrifice. The goat was slain and its blood taken into the Holy of Holies and sprinkled on the mercy seat, that golden cover on the ark of the covenant. This sprinkled blood covered the two tables of the Law inside the ark. The shed blood met (temporarily) the righteous demands of a holy God.

The priest then put his hands on the head of the other goat and confessed the sins of the people. Then the goat was taken out into the wilderness and set free to symbolize the carrying away of sins. "As far as the east is from the west, so far hath He removed our transgressions from us" (Ps. 103:12). In the Old Testament period, the blood of animals could never take away sin; it could only cover it until the time when Jesus would come and purchase a finished salvation. God had "passed over the sins that were past (Rom. 3:25, literal translation), knowing that His Son would come and finish the work. Because of His death and resurrection, there would be "redemption"—a purchasing of the sinner and setting him free.

Dr. G. Campbell Morgan was trying to explain "free salvation" to a coal miner, but the man was unable to understand it. "I have to pay for it," he kept arguing. With a flash of divine insight, Dr. Morgan asked, "How did you get down into the mine this morning?" "Why, it was easy," the man replied. "I just got on the elevator and went down."

Then Morgan asked, "Wasn't that too easy? Didn't it cost you something?"

The man laughed. "No, it didn't cost me anything; but it must have cost the company plenty to install that elevator." Then the man saw the truth: "It doesn't cost *me* anything to be saved, but it cost *God* the life of His Son."

f. *In perfect justice* (3:25a-26)—God must be perfectly consistent with Himself. He cannot break His own Law or violate His own nature. "God is love" (1 John 4:8), and "God is light" (1 John 1:5). A God of love wants to forgive sinners, but a God of holiness must punish sin and uphold His righteous Law. How can God be both "just and the justifier"? The answer is in Jesus Christ. When Jesus suffered the wrath of God on the Cross for the sins of the world, He fully met the demands of God's Law, *and also fully expressed the love of God's heart.* The animal sacrifices in the Old Testament never took away sin; but when Jesus died, He reached all the way back to Adam and took care of those sins. No one (including Satan) could accuse God of being unjust or unfair because of His seeming passing over of sins in the Old Testament time.

g. *To establish the Law* (3:27-31)—Because of his Jewish readers, Paul wanted to say more about the relationship of the Gospel to the Law. The doctrine of justification by faith is not against the Law, because it establishes the Law. God obeyed His own Law in working out the plan of salvation. Jesus in His life and death completely fulfilled the demands of the Law. God does not have two ways of salvation, one for the Jews and one for the Gentiles; for He is one God. He is consistent with His own nature and His own Law. If salvation is through the Law, then men can boast; but the principle of faith makes it impossible for men to boast. The swimmer, when he is saved from drowning, does not brag because he trusted the lifeguard. What else could he do? When a believing sinner is justified by faith, he cannot boast of his faith, but he can boast in a wonderful Saviour.

In Romans chapters 4 through 8, Paul explained how God's great plan of salvation was in complete harmony with the Old Testament Scriptures. He began first with the father of the Jewish nation, Abraham.

2. Justification Illustrated (4:1-25)

The Jewish Christians in Rome would immediately have asked, "How does this doctrine of justification by faith relate to our history? Paul, you say that this doctrine is witnessed to by the Law and the prophets. Well, what about Abraham?"

Paul accepted the challenge and explained how Abraham was saved. Abraham was called "our father," referring primarily to the Jews' natural and physical descent from Abraham. But in verse 11, Abraham was also called "the father of all them that believe," meaning, all who have trusted Christ.

(See Gal. 3:1-18.) Paul stated three important facts about Abraham's salvation that prove that the patriarch's spiritual experience was like that of believers today.

a. *He was justified by faith, not works* (4:1-8)— Paul called two witnesses to prove that statement: Moses (Gen. 15:6) and David (Ps. 32:1-2). In verses 1-3, Paul examined the experience of Abraham as recorded in Genesis 15. Abraham had defeated the kings (Gen. 14) and was wondering if they would return to fight again. God appeared to him and assured him that He was his shield and "exceeding great reward." But the thing that Abraham wanted most was a son and heir. God had promised him a son, but as yet the promise had not been fulfilled.

It was then that God told him to look at the stars. "So shall thy seed [descendants] be!" God promised; *and Abraham believed God's promise*. The Hebrew word translated *believed* means "to say amen." God gave a promise, and Abraham responded with "Amen!" It was this faith that was counted for righteousness.

The word *counted* in Romans 4:3 is a Greek word that means "to put to one's account." It is a banking term. This same word is used eleven times in this chapter, translated "reckoned" (4, 9-10) and "imputed" (6, 8, 11, 21-24), as well as "counted." When a man works, he earns a salary and this money is put to his account. But Abraham did not work for his salvation; he simply trusted God's Word. It was Jesus Christ who did the work on the Cross, and His righteousness was put on Abraham's account.

Verse 5 makes a startling statement: God justifies *the ungodly!* The Law said, "I will not justify the wicked" (Ex. 23:7). The Old Testament judge was commanded to "justify the righteous, and condemn the wicked" (Deut. 25:1). When Solomon dedicated the temple, he asked God to condemn the wicked and justify the righteous (1 Kings 8:31-32)! But God justifies the ungodly—*because there are no godly for Him to justify!* He put our sins on Christ's account that He might put Christ's righteousness on our account.

In verses 6 through 8, Paul used David as a witness, quoting from one of David's psalms of confession after his terrible sin with Bathsheba (Ps. 32:1-2). David made two amazing statements: (1) God forgives sins and imputes righteousness apart from works, (2) God does not impute our sins. In other words, once we are justified, our record contains Christ's perfect righteousness *and can never again contain our sins.* Christians do sin, and these sins need to be forgiven if we are to have fellowship with God (1 John 1:5-7); *but these sins are not held against us.* God does keep a record of our works, so that He might reward us when Jesus comes; but He is not keeping a record of our sins.

b. *He was justified by grace, not Law* (4:9-17)— As we have seen, the Jews gloried in circumcision and the Law. If a Jew was to become righteous before God, he would have to be circumcised and obey the Law. Paul had already made it clear in Romans 2:12-29 that there must be an *inward* obedience to the Law, and a "circumcision of the heart." Mere external observances can never save the lost sinner.

But Abraham was declared righteous when he was in the state of uncircumcision. From the Jewish point of view, Abraham was a Gentile. Abraham was 99 years old when he was circumcised (Gen. 17:23-27). This was more than 14 years after the events in Genesis 15. The conclusion is obvious: circumcision had nothing to do with his justification.

Then why was circumcision given? It was a sign and a seal (Rom. 4:11). As a sign, it was evidence that he belonged to God and believed His promise. As a seal, it was a reminder to him that God had given the promise and would keep it. Believers today are sealed by the Holy Spirit of God (Eph. 1:13-14). They have also experienced a spiritual circumcision in the heart (Col. 2:10-12), not just a minor physical operation, but the putting off of the old nature through the death and resurrection of Christ. Circumcision did not add to Abraham's salvation; it merely attested to it.

But Abraham was also justified before the Law was given, and this fact Paul discusses in verses 13 through 17. The key word here is "promise." Abraham was justified by believing God's promise, not by obeying God's Law; for God's Law through Moses had not yet been given. The promise to Abraham was given purely through God's grace. Abraham did not earn it or merit it. So today, God justifies the ungodly because they believe His gracious promise, not because they obey His Law. The Law was not given to save men, but to show men that they need to be saved (Rom. 4:15).

The fact that Abraham was justified by grace and not Law proves that salvation is for all men. Abraham is the father of all believers, both Jews and Gentiles. (Rom. 4:16; Gal. 3:7, 29.) Instead of the Jew complaining because Abraham was not saved by Law, he ought to rejoice that God's salvation is available to all men, and that Abraham has a spiritual family (all true believers) as well as a physical family (the nation of Israel). Paul saw this as a fulfillment of Genesis 17:5: "I have made thee a father of many nations."·

c. *He was justified by Resurrection power, not human effort* (4:18-25)—These verses are an expansion of one phrase in verse 17: "who quickeneth the dead." Paul saw the rejuvenation of Abraham's body as a picture of resurrection from the dead; and then he related it to the resurrection of Christ.

One reason why God delayed in sending Abraham and Sarah a son was to permit all their natural strength to decline and then disappear. It was unthinkable that a man 99 years old could beget a child in the womb of his wife who was 89 years old! From a reproductive point of view, both of them were dead.

But Abraham did not walk by sight; he walked by faith. What God promises, He performs. All we need do is believe. Abraham's initial faith in God as recorded in Genesis 15 did not diminish in the years that followed. In Genesis 17 and 18, Abraham was "strong in faith." It was this faith that gave him strength to beget a son in his old age.

The application to salvation is clear: God must wait until the sinner is "dead" and unable to help himself before He can release His saving power. As long as the lost sinner thinks he is strong enough to do anything to please God, he cannot be saved by grace. It was when Abraham admitted that he was "dead" that God's power went to work in his body. It is when the lost sinner confesses that he is spiritually dead and unable to help himself that God can save him.

The Gospel is "the power of God unto salvation" (Rom. 1:16) because of the resurrection of Jesus Christ from the dead. Romans 4:24 and Romans

10:9-10 parallel each other. Jesus Christ was "delivered up to die on account of our offenses, and was raised up because of our justification" (Rom. 4:25, literal translation). This means that the resurrection of Christ is the proof that God accepted His Son's sacrifice, and that now sinners can be justified without God violating His own Law or contradicting His own nature.

The key, of course, is "if we believe" (v. 24). There are over 60 references to faith or unbelief in Romans. God's saving power is experienced by those who believe in Christ (Rom. 1:16). His righteousness is given to those who believe (Rom. 3:22). We are justified by faith (Rom. 5:1). The object of our faith is Jesus Christ who died for us and rose again.

All of these facts make Abraham's faith that much more wonderful. He did not have a Bible to read; he had only the simple promise of God. He was almost alone as a believer, surrounded by heathen unbelievers. He could not look back at a long record of faith; in fact, he was helping to write that record. Yet Abraham believed God. People today have a complete Bible to read and study. They have a church fellowship, and can look back at centuries of faith as recorded in church history and the Bible. Yet many refuse to believe!

Dr. Harry Ironside, for 18 years pastor of the Moody Church in Chicago, told of visiting a Sunday School class while on vacation. The teacher asked, "How were people saved in Old Testament times?"

After a pause, one man replied, "By keeping the Law." "That's right," said the teacher.

But Dr. Ironside interrupted: "My Bible says that by the deeds of the Law shall no flesh be justified."

The teacher was a bit embarrassed, so he said, "Well, does somebody else have an idea?"

Another student replied, "They were saved by bringing sacrifices to God."

"Yes, that's right!" the teacher said, and tried to go on with the lesson.

But Dr. Ironside interrupted, "My Bible says that the blood of bulls and goats cannot take away sin."

By this time the unprepared teacher was sure the visitor knew more about the Bible than he did, so he said, "Well, *you* tell us how people were saved in the Old Testament!"

And Dr. Ironside explained that they were saved by faith—the same way people are saved today! Twenty-one times in Hebrews 11 you find the same words "by faith."

If you are a Jew, you are a child of Abraham physically; but are you a child of Abraham *spiritually?* Abraham is the father of all who believe on Jesus Christ and are justified by faith. If you are a Gentile, you can never be a natural descendant of Abraham; but you can be one of his *spiritual* descendants. Abraham "believed God and it was counted unto him for righteousness."

Romans 5:1-21

Therefore being justified by faith, we have peace with God through our Lord Jesus Christ: [2] By whom also we have access by faith into this grace wherein we stand, and rejoice in hope of the glory of God. [3] And not only so, but we glory in tribulations also: knowing that tribulation worketh patience; [4] And patience, experience; and experience, hope: [5] And hope maketh not ashamed; because the love of God is shed abroad in our hearts by the Holy Ghost which is given unto us. [6] For when we were yet without strength, in due time Christ died for the ungodly.   (Romans 5:1-6)
12 Wherefore, as by one man sin entered into the world, and death by sin; and so death passed upon all men, for that all have sinned: [13] (For until the law sin was in the world: but sin is not imputed when there is no law. [14] Nevertheless death reigned from Adam to Moses, even over them that had not sinned after the similitude of Adam's transgression, who is the figure of Him that was to come . . .)
(Romans 5:12-14)
20 Moreover the law entered, that the offense might abound. But where sin abounded, grace did much more abound: [21] That as sin hath reigned unto death, even so might grace reign through righteousness unto eternal life by Jesus Christ our Lord.   (Romans 5:20-21)

4

Live Like a King!

Since Romans is a book of logic, it is a book of "therefores." We have the "therefore" of *condemnation* in 3:20, *justification* in 5:1, *no condemnation* in 8:1, and *dedication* in 12:1. In presenting his case, Paul has proved that the whole world is guilty before God, and that no one can be saved by religious deeds, such as keeping the Law. He has explained that God's way of salvation has always been "by grace, through faith" (Eph. 2:8-9), and he has used Abraham as his illustration. If a reader of the letter stopped at this point, he would know that he *needed* to and *could* be saved.

But there is much more the sinner needs to know about justification by faith. Can he be sure that it will last? How is it possible for God to save a sinner through the death of Christ on the cross? Chapter 5 is Paul's explanation of the last two words in chapter 4: "our justification." He explained two basic truths: the blessings of our justification (5:1-11), and the basis for our justification (5:12-21).

1. The Blessings of our Justification (5:1-11)

In listing these blessings, Paul accomplished two purposes. First, he told how wonderful it is to be a Christian. Our justification is not simply a guarantee of heaven, as thrilling as that is, but it is also the source of tremendous blessings that we enjoy here and now.

His second purpose was to assure his readers that justification is a lasting thing. His Jewish readers in particular would ask, "Can this spiritual experience last if it does not require obedience to the Law?" What about the trials and sufferings of life? What about the coming judgment?" When God declared us righteous in Jesus Christ, He gave to us seven spiritual blessings that assure us that we cannot be lost.

a. *Peace with God* (5:1)—The unsaved person is at "enmity with God" (Rom. 5:10; 8:7) because he cannot obey God's Law or fulfill God's will. Two verses from Isaiah make the matter clear: "There is no peace, saith the Lord, unto the wicked" (48:22); "And the work of righteousness shall be peace" (32:17). Condemnation means that God declares us *sinners,* which is a declaration of *war.* Justification means that God declares us *righteous,* which is a declaration of *peace,* made possible by Christ's death on the cross. "Mercy and truth are met together; righteousness and peace have kissed each other" (Ps. 85:10). "Because the law worketh wrath" (Rom. 4:15), nobody condemned by the Law can enjoy peace with God. But when you are justified by faith, you are declared righteous, and the Law cannot condemn you or declare war!

b. *Access to God* (5:2a)—The Jew was kept from God's presence by the veil in the temple; and the Gentile was kept out by a wall in the temple with a warning on it that any Gentile who went beyond would be killed. But when Jesus died, He tore the veil (Luke 23:45) and broke down the wall (Eph. 2:14). In Christ, believing Jews and Gentiles have access to God (Eph. 2:18; Heb. 10:19-25); and they can draw upon the inexhaustible riches of the grace of God (Eph. 1:7; 2:4; 3:8). We stand "in grace" and not "in Law." Justification has to do with our standing; sanctification has to do with our state. The child of a king can enter his father's presence no matter how the child looks. The word "access" here means "entrance to the king through the favor of another."

c. *Glorious hope* (5:2b)—"Peace with God" takes care of the past: He will no longer hold our sins against us. "Access to God" takes care of the present: we can come to Him at any time for the help we need. "Hope of the glory of God" takes care of the future: one day we shall share in His glory! The word "rejoice" can be translated "boast," not only in verse 2, but also in verses 3 and 11 ("joy"). When we were sinners, there was nothing to boast about (Rom. 3:27), because we fell short of the glory of God (Rom. 3:23). But in Christ, we boast in *His* righteousness and glory! Paul will amplify this in Romans 8:18-30.

d. *Christian character* (5:3-4)—Justification is no escape from the trials of life. "In this world ye shall have tribulation" (John 16:33). But for the believer, trials work *for* him and not *against* him. No amount of suffering can separate us from the Lord (Rom. 8:35-39); instead, trials bring us closer to the Lord and make us more like the Lord. Suffering builds Christian character. The word "experience" in verse 4 means "character that has been proved." The sequence is: tribulation—patience—proven character—hope. Our English word "tribulation" comes from a Latin word *tribulum.* In Paul's day, a *tribulum* was a heavy piece of timber with spikes in it, used for threshing the grain. The *tribulum* was drawn over the grain and it separated the wheat from the chaff. As we go through tribulations, and depend on God's grace, the trials only purify us and help to get rid of the chaff.

e. *God's love within* (5:5-8)—"Hope deferred maketh the heart sick" (Prov. 13:12). But as we wait for this hope to be fulfilled, the love of God is "poured out into our hearts" (literal translation). Note how the first three of the "fruit of the Spirit" are experienced: love (v. 5), joy (v. 2), and peace (v. 1). Before we were saved, God proved His love by sending Christ to die for us. Now that we are His children, surely He will love us more. It is the inner experience of this love through the Spirit that sustains us as we go through tribulations.

For many months I visited a young man in a hospital who had almost burned to death. I do not know how many operations and skin grafts he had during those months, or how many specialists visited him. But the thing that sustained him during those difficult months was not the explanations of the doctors but the promises they gave him that he would recover. That was his hope. And the thing that sustained his hope was the love of his family and many friends as they stood by him. The love of God was channeled through them to him. He did recover and today gives glory to God.

Faith (v. 1), hope (v. 2), and love (v. 5) all combine to give the believer patience in the trials of life. And patience makes it possible for the believer to grow in character and become a mature child of God (James 1:1-4).

f. *Salvation from future wrath* (5:9-10)—Paul argued from the lesser to the greater. If God saved us when we were enemies, surely He will keep on saving us now that we are His children. There is a "wrath to come," but no true believer will experience it (1 Thes. 1:9-10; 5:8-10). Paul further argued that if Christ's *death* accomplished so much for us, how much more will He do for us in His *life* as He intercedes for us in heaven! "Saved by His life" refers to Romans 4:25: "raised again for [on account of] our justification." Because He lives, we are eternally saved (Heb. 7:23-25).

A will is of no effect until the death of the one who wrote it. Then an executor takes over and sees to it that the will is obeyed and the inheritance distributed. But suppose the executor is unscrupulous and wants to get the inheritance for himself? He may figure out many devious ways to circumvent the law and steal the inheritance.

Jesus Christ wrote us into His will, and He wrote the will with His blood. "This cup is the new testament in my blood, which is shed for you" (Luke 22:20). He died so that the will would be in force; but then He arose from the dead and returned to heaven that He might enforce the will Himself and distribute the inheritance. Thus, we are "saved by His life."

g. *Reconciliation with God* (5:11)—The word "atonement" means "reconciliation, brought back into fellowship with God." The term is mentioned also in verse 10. In Romans 1:18-32, Paul explained how men declared war on God and, because of this, deserved to be condemned eternally. But God did not declare war on man. Instead, He sent His Son as the Peacemaker (Eph. 2:11-18) that men might be reconciled to God.

A review of these seven blessings of justification shows how certain our salvation is in Christ. Totally apart from Law, and purely by grace, we have a salvation that takes care of the past, the present, and the future. Christ died for us; Christ lives for us; Christ is coming for us! Hallelujah, what a Saviour!

2. The Basis of Our Justification (5:12-21)

How is it possible for God to save sinners in the Person of Jesus Christ? We understand that somehow Christ took our place on the cross, but how was such a substitution possible?

Paul answered the question in this section, and these verses are the very heart of the letter. To understand these verses a few general truths about this section need to be understood. First, note the repetition of the little word *one.* It is used eleven times. The key idea here is our identification with Adam and with Christ. Second, note the repetition of the word *reign* which is used five times. Paul saw two men—Adam and Christ—each of them reigning over a kingdom. Finally, note that the phrase *much more* is repeated five times. This means that in Jesus Christ we have gained much more than we ever lost in Adam!

In short, this section is a contrast of Adam and Christ. Adam was given dominion over the old creation, he sinned, and he lost his kingdom. Because of Adam's sin, all mankind is under condemnation and death. Christ came as the King over a new creation (2 Cor. 5:17). By His obedience on the Cross, He brought in righteousness and justification. Christ not only undid all the damage that Adam's sin effected, but He accomplished "much more" by making us the very sons of God. Some of this "much more" Paul has already explained in Romans 5:1-11.

Skeptics sometimes ask, "Was it fair for God to condemn the whole world just because of one man's disobedience?" The answer, of course, is that it was not only fair; but it was also wise and gracious. To begin with, if God had tested each human being individually, the result would have been the same: disobedience. But even more important, by condemning the human race through one man (Adam), God was then *able to save the human race through One Man* (Jesus Christ)! Each of us is racially united to Adam, so that his deed affects us. (See Heb. 7:9-10 for an example of this racial headship.) The fallen angels cannot be saved because they are not a race. They sinned individually and were judged individually. There can be no representative to take their judgment for them and save them. But because you and I were lost in Adam, our *racial* head, we can be saved in Christ, the Head of the new creation. God's plan was both gracious and wise.

Our final question must be answered: how do we know that we are racially united to Adam? The answer is in Romans 5:12-14, and the argument runs like this: We know that all men die. But death is the result of disobeying the Law. There was no Law from Adam to Moses, but men still died. A general result demands a general cause. What is that cause? It can be only one thing: the disobedience of Adam. When Adam sinned, he ultimately died. All of his descendants died (Gen. 5), yet the Law had not yet been given. Conclusion: they died because of Adam's sin. "For that all have sinned" (v. 12) means "all have sinned *in Adam's sin*." Men do not die because of their own acts of sin; otherwise, babies would not die (Rom. 9:11). Men die because they are united racially to Adam, and "in Adam all men die" (1 Cor. 15:22).

Having understood these general truths about the passage, we may now examine the contrasts that Paul gives between Adam and Christ and between Adam's sin and Christ's act of obedience on the Cross.

a. *Adam's offense is contrasted with Christ's free gift* (5:15)—Because of Adam's trespass, many died; because of Christ's obedience the grace of God abounds to many bringing life. The word "many" (literally "the many") means the same as "all men" in verses 12 and 18. Note the "much more"; for the grace of Christ brings not only physical life, but also spiritual life and abundant life. Christ did conquer death and one day will raise the bodies of all who have died "in Christ." If He stopped there, He would only reverse the effects of Adam's sin; but He went on to do "much more." He gives eternal life abundantly to all who trust Him (John 10:10).

b. *The effect of Adam's sin is contrasted with the effect of Christ's obedience* (5:16)—Adam's sin brought judgment and condemnation; but Christ's work on the cross brings justification. When Adam sinned, he was declared unrighteous and condemned. When a sinner trusts Christ, he is justified —declared righteous in Christ.

c. *The two "reigns" are contrasted* (5:17)—Because of Adam's disobedience, death reigned. Read the "book of the generations of Adam" in Genesis 5, and note the solemn repetition of the phrase "and he died." In verse 14, Paul argued that men did not die "from Adam to Moses" for the same reason that Adam died—breaking a revealed law of God—for the Law had not yet been given. "The wages of sin is death" (Rom. 6:23a). Because *sin* was reigning in men's lives (Rom. 5:21), *death* was also reigning (vv. 14 and 17).

But in Jesus Christ we enter a new kingdom: "For the kingdom of God is not meat and drink; but *righteousness,* and *peace,* and *joy* in the Holy Ghost" (Rom. 14:17. "Therefore being justified by faith" we are declared *righteous,* we have *peace* with God, and we *rejoice* in the hope of the glory of God. Note that it is *we* who reign! "Much more they . . . shall reign in life by one, Jesus Christ." In Adam we lost our kingship, but in Jesus Christ we reign as kings. And we reign "much more"! Our spiritual reign is far greater than Adam's earthly reign, for we share "abundance of grace and of the gift of righteousness" (Rom. 5:17).

d. *The two "one acts" are contrasted* (5:18-19) —Adam did not have to commit a series of sins. In one act God tested Adam, and he failed. It is termed an "offense" and an act of "disobedience." The word *offense* means "trespass—crossing over the line." God told Adam how far he could go, and Adam decided to go beyond the appointed limit. "Of every tree of the garden thou mayest freely eat: but of the tree of the knowledge of good and evil, thou shalt not eat of it: for in the day that thou eatest thereof, thou shalt surely die" (Gen. 2:16-17).

In contrast to "the trespass of one" is "the righteousness of one," meaning the righteous work of Christ on the Cross. In verse 19 Paul calls it "the obedience of one" (see Phil. 2:5-12). Christ's sacrifice on the Cross not only made possible "justification," but also "justification *of life*" (italics mine). Justication is not merely a legal term that describes our position before God ("just as if I'd never sinned"); but it results in a certain kind of life. "Justification of life" in verse 18 is parallel to "be made righteous" in verse 19. In other words, our justification is the result of a living union with Christ. And this union ought to result in a new kind of life, a righteous life of obedience to God. Our union with Adam made us sinners; our union with Christ enables us to "reign in life."

e. *Law and grace are contrasted* (5:20-21)— "Then law crept in . . ." (Charles B. Williams translation); or, "Then the law came in beside . . ." (literal translation). Grace was not an addition to God's plan; grace was a part of God's plan from the very beginning. God dealt with Adam and Eve in grace; He dealt with the patriarchs in grace; and He dealt with the nation of Israel in grace. He gave the Law through Moses, not to replace His grace, but to reveal man's need for grace. Law was temporary, but grace is eternal.

But as the Law made man's sins increase, God's grace abounded even more. God's grace was more than adequate to deal with man's sins. Even though sin and death still reign in this world, God's grace is also reigning through the righteousness of Christ. The Christian's body is subject to death and his old nature tempts him to sin; but in Jesus Christ, he can "reign in life" because he is a part of the gracious kingdom of Christ.

An Old Testament story helps us understand the conflict between these two "reigns" in the world today. God rejected Saul as the king of Israel, and anointed David. Those who trusted David eventually shared his kingdom of peace and joy. Those who trusted Saul ended in shame and defeat.

Like David, Jesus Christ is God's anointed King.

Like Saul, Satan is still free to work in this world and seek to win men's allegiance. Sin and death are reigning in the "old creation" over which Adam was the head, but grace and righteousness are reigning in "the new creation" over which Christ is the Head. And as we yield to Him, we "reign in life."

In verse 14, Adam is called "the figure of Him that was to come." Adam was a type, or picture, of Jesus Christ. Adam came from the earth, but Jesus is the Lord from heaven (1 Cor. 15:47). Adam was tested in a garden, surrounded by beauty and love; Jesus was tempted in a wilderness, and He died on a cruel cross surrounded by hatred and ugliness. Adam was a thief, and was cast out of Paradise; but Jesus Christ turned to a thief and said, "Today shalt thou be with Me in Paradise" (Luke 23:43). The Old Testament is "the book of the generations of Adam" (Gen. 5:1) and it ends with "a curse" (Mal. 4:6). The New Testament is "The book of the generation of Jesus Christ" (Matt. 1:1) and it ends with "no more curse" (Rev. 22:3).

You cannot help being "in Adam," for this came by your first birth over which you had no control. But you can help staying "in Adam," for you can experience a second birth—a new birth from above —that will put you "in Christ." This is why Jesus said "Ye must be born again" (John 3:7).

Romans 6:1-23

What shall we say then? Shall we continue in sin, that grace may abound? ² God forbid. How shall we, that are dead to sin, live any longer therein? ³ Know ye not, that as many of us as were baptized into Jesus Christ were baptized into His death? ⁴ Therefore we are buried with Him in baptism into death: that like as Christ was raised up from the dead by the glory of the Father, even so we also should walk in newness of life. ⁵ For if we have been planted together in the likeness of His death, we shall be also in the likeness of His resurrection: ⁶ Knowing this, that our old man is crucified with Him, that the body of sin might be destroyed, that henceforth we should not serve sin. ⁷ For he that is dead is freed from sin. (Romans 6:1-7)

13 Neither yield ye your members as instruments of unrighteousness unto sin: but yield yourselves unto God, as those that are alive from the dead, and your members as instruments of righteousness unto God. ¹⁴ For sin shall not have dominion over you: for ye are not under the law, but under grace. (Romans 6:13-14)

20 For when ye were the servants of sin, ye were free from righteousness. ²¹ What fruit had ye then in those things whereof ye are now ashamed? for the end of those things is death. ²² But now being made free from sin, and become servants to God, ye have your fruit unto holiness, and the end everlasting life. ²³ For the wages of sin is death; but the gift of God is eternal life through Jesus Christ our Lord. (Romans 6:20-23)

5

Dying to Live

During a court session, an attorney will often rise to his feet and say, "Your Honor, I object!" Some of the Roman Christians must have felt like objecting as they heard Paul's letter being read, and Paul seemed to anticipate their thinking. In chapters 6 through 8 Paul defended his doctrine of justification by faith. He anticipated three objections: (1) "If God's grace abounds when we sin, then let's continue sinning so we might experience more grace" (6:1-14); (2) "If we are no longer under the Law, then we are free to live as we please" (6:15—7:6); and (3) "You have made God's Law sinful" (7:7-25).

These objections prove that the readers did not understand either Law or grace. They were going to extremes: legalism on the one hand and license on the other. So as Paul defended justification he also explained sanctification. He told how we can live lives of *victory* (chap. 6), *liberty* (chap. 7), and *security* (chap. 8). He explained our relationship to the flesh, the Law, and the Holy Spirit. In chapter 6, Paul gave three instructions for attaining victory over sin.

1. Know (6:1-10)

The repetition of the word "know" in verses 1, 6, and 9 indicates that Paul wanted us to understand a basic doctrine. Christian living depends on Christian learning; duty is always founded on doctrine. If Satan can keep a Christian ignorant, he can keep him impotent.

The basic truth Paul was teaching is the believer's identification with Christ in death, burial, and resurrection. Just as we are identified with Adam in sin and condemnation, so we are now identified with Christ in righteousness and justification. At Romans 5:12, Paul made a transition from discussing "sins" to discussing "sin"—from the actions to the principle, from the fruit to the root. Jesus Christ not only died for our sins, but He also died unto sin, and we died with Him. Perhaps a chart will explain the contrasts better.

Romans 3:21—5:21	Romans 6—8
Substitution: He died for me	Identification: I died with Him
He died *for* my sins	He died *unto* sin
He paid sin's penalty	He broke sin's power
Justification: righteousness imputed (put to my account)	Sanctification: righteousness imparted (made a part of my life)
Saved by His death	Saved by His life

In other words, justification by faith is not simply a legal matter between me and God; it is a living relationship. It is "a justification which brings life" (Rom. 5:18, literal translation). I am in Christ" and identified with Him. Therefore, whatever happened to Christ has happened to me. When He died, I died. When He arose, I arose in Him. I am now seated with Him in the heavenlies! (See Eph. 2:1-10; Col. 3:1-3.) Because of this living union with Christ, the believer has a totally new relationship to sin.

a. *He is dead to sin* (6:2-5)—Paul's illustration is baptism. The Greek word has two basic meanings: (1) a literal meaning—to dip or immerse; and (2) a figurative meaning—to be identified with. An example of the latter would be 1 Corinthians 10:2: "And were all baptized unto Moses in the cloud and in the sea." The nation of Israel was identified with Moses as their leader when they crossed the Red Sea.

It appears that Paul had both the literal and the figurative in mind in this paragraph, for he used the readers' experience of water baptism to remind them of their identification with Christ through the baptism of the Holy Spirit. To be "baptized into Jesus Christ" (v. 3) is the same as "For by one Spirit are we all baptized into one body" (1 Cor. 12:13). There is a difference between water baptism and the baptism of the Spirit (John 1:33). When a sinner trusts Christ, he is immediately born into the family of God and receives the gift of the Holy Spirit. A good illustration of this is the household of Cornelius when they heard Peter preach (Acts 10:34-48). When these people believed on Christ, they immediately received the Holy Spirit. And *then* they were baptized. Peter's words "Whosoever believeth in him shall receive remission of sins" gave to them the promise that they needed. They believed—and they were saved!

Historians agree that the mode of baptism in the Early Church was immersion. The believer was "buried" in the water and brought up again as a picture of death, burial, and resurrection. Baptism by immersion (which is the illustration Paul is using in Romans 6) pictures the believer's identification with Christ in His death, burial, and resurrection. It is an outward symbol of an inward experience. Paul is not saying that their immersion in water put them "into Jesus Christ," for that was accomplished by the Spirit when they believed. Their immersion was a picture of what the Spirit did: the Holy Spirit identified them with Christ in His death, burial, and resurrection.

This means that the believer has a new relationship to sin. He is "dead to sin." "I am crucified with Christ . . ." (Gal. 2:20). If a drunk dies, he can no longer be tempted by alcohol because his body is dead to all physical senses. He cannot see the alcohol, smell it, taste it, or desire it. In Jesus Christ we have died to sin so that we no longer want to "continue in sin." But we are not only dead to sin; we are also alive in Christ. We have been raised from the dead and now walk in the power of His resurrection. We walk in "newness of life" because we share His life. "I am crucified with Christ, nevertheless I live" (Gal. 2:20).

This tremendous spiritual truth is illustrated in the miracle of the resurrection of Lazarus (John 11). When Jesus arrived at Bethany, Lazarus had been in the tomb four days; so there was no question about his death. By the power of His Word ("Lazarus, come forth!") Jesus raised His friend from the dead. But when Lazarus appeared at the door of the tomb, he was wrapped in graveclothes. So Jesus commanded, "Loose him, and let him go!" He had been raised to walk "in newness of life." In John 12, Lazarus was seated with Christ at the table, in fellowship with Him. Dead—raised from the dead—set free to walk in newness of life— seated with Christ: all of these facts illustrate the spiritual truths of our identification with Christ as given in Ephesians 2:1-10.

Too many Christians are "betweeners": they live between Egypt and Canaan, saved but never satisfied; or they live between Good Friday and Easter, believing in the Cross but not entering into the power and glory of the Resurrection. Verse 5 indicates that our union with Christ assures our future resurrection should we die. But verse 4 teaches that we share His resurrection power *today.* "Since, then, you have been raised with Christ, set your hearts on things above . . . For you died, and your life is now hidden with Christ in God" (Col. 3:1, 3, NIV).

It is clear, then, that the believer cannot deliberately live in sin since he has a new relationship to sin because of his identification with Christ. The believer has died to the old life; he has been raised to enjoy a new life. The believer does not want to go back into sin any more than Lazarus wanted to go back into the tomb dressed again in his graveclothes! Then Paul introduced a second fact:

b. *He should not serve sin* (6:6-10)—Sin is a terrible master, and it finds a willing servant in the human body. The body is not sinful; the body is neutral. It can be controlled either by sin or by God. But man's fallen nature, which is not changed at conversion, gives sin a beachhead from which it can attack and then control. Paul expressed the problem: "For I know that in me (that is, in my flesh) dwelleth no good thing: for to will is present with me; but how to perform that which is good I find not" (Rom. 7:18).

A tremendous fact is introduced here: the old man (the old ego, self) was crucified with Christ so that the body need not be controlled by sin. The word "destroyed" in verse 6 does not mean annihilated; it means "rendered inactive, made of no effect." The same Greek word is translated "loosed" in Romans 7:2. If a woman's husband dies, she is "loosed" from the law of her husband and is free to marry again. There is a change in relationship. The law is still there, but it has no authority over the woman because her husband is dead.

Sin wants to be our master. It finds a foothold in the old nature, and through the old nature seeks to control the members of the body. But in Jesus Christ, we died to sin; and the old nature was crucified so that the old life is rendered inoperative. Paul was not describing an experience; he was stating a fact. The practical experience was to come later. It is a fact of history that Jesus Christ died on the cross. It is also a fact of history that the believer died with Him; and "he that is dead is freed from sin" (v. 7). Not "free *to* sin" as Paul's accusers falsely stated; but "freed from sin."

Sin and death have no dominion over Christ. We are "in Christ"; therefore, sin and death have no dominion over us. Jesus Christ not only died "for sin," but He also died "unto sin." That is, He not only paid the penalty for sin, but He broke the power of sin. This idea of dominion takes us back to Romans 5:12-21 where Paul dealt with the "reigns" of sin, death, and grace. Through Christ we "reign in life" (Rom. 5:17) so that sin no longer controls our lives.

The big question now is, "I believe the facts of history; but how do I make this work in daily experience?" This leads to Paul's second instruction.

2. Reckon (6:11)

In some parts of the United States, "to reckon" means "to think" or "to guess." "I reckon" is also the equivalent of "I suppose." But none of these popular meanings can apply to this verse. The word *reckon* is a translation of a Greek word that is used 41 times in the New Testament—19 times in Romans alone. It appears in Romans 4 where it is translated as "count, reckon, impute." It means "to take into account, to calculate, to estimate." The word *impute*—"to put to one's account"—is perhaps the best translation.

To reckon means "to put to one's account." It simply means to believe that what God says is true in His Word is really true in your life.

Paul didn't tell his readers to *feel* as if they were dead to sin, or even to *understand* it fully, but to act upon God's Word and claim it for themselves. Reckoning is a matter of faith that issues in action. It is like endorsing a check: if we really believe that the money is in the checking account we will sign our name and collect the money. Reckoning is not claiming a promise, but acting upon a fact. God does not command us to become dead to sin. He tells us that we *are* dead to sin and alive unto God, and then commands us to act upon it. Even if we do not act upon it, the facts are still true.

Paul's first instruction ("know") centered in the *mind,* and this second instruction ("reckon") focuses on the *heart*. His third instruction touches the *will*.

3. Yield (6:12-23)

The word *yield* is found five times in this section (verses 13, 16, and 19), and means "to place at one's disposal, to present, to offer as a sacrifice." According to Romans 12:1, the believer's body should be presented to the Lord as "a living sacrifice" for His glory. The Old Testament sacrifices were dead sacrifices. The Lord may ask some of us to die for Him, but He asks all of us to *live* for Him.

a. *How we are to yield* (6:12-13)—This is an act of the will based on the knowledge we have of what Christ has done for us. It is an intelligent act—not the impulsive decision of the moment based on some emotional stirring. It is important to notice the tenses of the verbs in these verses. A literal translation is: "Do not constantly allow sin to reign in your mortal body so that you are constantly obeying its lusts. Neither constantly yield your members of your body as weapons [or tools] of unrighteousness to sin; but once and for all yield yourselves to God." That once-and-for-all surrender is described in Romans 12:1.

There must be in the believer's life that final and complete surrender of the body to Jesus Christ. This does not mean there will be no further steps of surrender, because there will be. The longer we walk with Christ, the deeper the fellowship must become. But there can be no subsequent steps without that first step. The tense of the verb in Romans 12:1 corresponds with that in Romans 6:13—a once-and-for-all yielding to the Lord. To be sure, we daily surrender afresh to Him; but even that is based on a final and complete surrender.

Why does the Lord want your body? To begin with, the believer's body is God's temple, and He wants to use it for His glory (1 Cor. 6:19-20; Phil. 1:20-21). But Paul wrote that the body is also God's tool and God's weapon (Rom. 6:13). God wants to use the members of the body as tools for building His kingdom and weapons for fighting His enemies.

The Bible tells of people who permitted God to take and use their bodies for the fulfilling of His purposes. God used the rod in Moses' hand and conquered Egypt. He used the sling in David's hand to defeat the Philistises. He used the mouths and tongues of the prophets. Paul's dedicated feet carried him from city to city as he proclaimed the Gospel. The Apostle John's eyes saw visions of the future, his ears heard God's message, and his fingers wrote it all down in a book that we can read.

But you can also read in the Bible accounts of the members of the body being used for sinful purposes. David's eyes looked upon his neighbor's wife; his mind plotted a wicked scheme; his hand signed a cowardly order for the woman's husband to be killed. As you read Psalm 51, you see that his whole body was affected by sin: his eyes (v. 3), mind (v. 6), ears (v. 8), heart (v. 10), and lips and mouth (vv. 14-15). No wonder he prayed for a *thorough* cleansing! (v. 2)

b. *Why we are to yield* (6:14-23)—Three words summarize the reasons for our yielding: *favor* (vv. 14-15), *freedom* (vv. 16-20), and *fruit* (vv. 21-23).

(1) *Favor* (6:14-15). It is because of God's grace that we yield ourselves to Him. Paul has proved that we are not saved by the Law and that we do not live under the Law. The fact that we are saved

by grace does not give us an excuse to sin; but it does give us a reason to obey. Sin and Law go together. "The sting of death is sin; and the strength of sin is the law" (1 Cor. 15:56). Since we are not under Law, but under grace, sin is robbed of its strength.

(2) *Freedom* (6:16-20). The illustration of the master and servant is obvious. Whatever you yield to becomes your master. Before you were saved, you were the slave of sin. Now that you belong to Christ, you are freed from that old slavery and made the servant of Christ. Verse 19 suggests that the Christian ought to be as enthusiastic in yielding to the Lord as he was in yielding to sin. A friend once said to me, "I want to be as good a saint as I was a sinner!" I knew what he meant because in his unconverted days he was almost "the chief of sinners."

The unsaved person is free—free *from* righteousness (v. 20). But his bondage to sin only leads him deeper into slavery so that it becomes harder and harder to do what is right. The Prodigal Son is an example of this (Luke 15:11-24). When he was at home, he decided he wanted his freedom, so he left home to find himself and enjoy himself. But his rebellion only led him deeper into slavery. He was the slave of wrong desires, then the slave of wrong deeds; and finally he became a literal slave when he took care of the pigs. He wanted to find himself, but he lost himself! What he thought was freedom turned out to be the worst kind of slavery. It was only when he returned home and *yielded to his father* that he found true freedom.

(3) *Fruit* (6:21-23). If you serve a master, you can expect to receive wages. Sin pays wages—death! God also pays wages—holiness and ever-

lasting life. In the old life, we produced fruit that made us ashamed. In the new life in Christ, we produce fruit that glorifies God and brings joy to our lives. We usually apply verse 23 to the lost, and certainly it does apply; but it also has a warning for the saved. (After all, it was written to Christians.) "There is a sin unto death" (1 John 5:17). "For this reason many among you are weak and sick, and a number sleep" (1 Cor. 11:30). Samson, for example, would not yield himself to God, but preferred to yield to the lusts of the flesh, and the result was death (Jud. 16). If the believer refuses to surrender his body to the Lord, but uses its members for sinful purposes, then he is in danger of being disciplined by the Father, and this could mean death. (See Hebrews 12:5-11, and note the end of verse 9 in particular.)

These three instructions need to be heeded each day that we live. KNOW that you have been crucified with Christ and are dead to sin. RECKON this fact to be true in your own life. YIELD your body to the Lord to be used for His glory.

Now that you KNOW these truths, RECKON them to be true in *your* life, and then YIELD yourself to God.

Romans 7:1-25

Know ye not, brethren, (for I speak to them that know the law,) how that the law hath dominion over a man as long as he liveth? [2] For the woman which hath an husband is bound by the law to her husband so long as he liveth; but if the husband be dead, she is loosed from the law of her husband. [3] So then if, while her husband liveth, she be married to another man, she shall be called an adulteress: but if her husband be dead, she is free from that law; so that she is no adulteress, though she be married to another man. [4] Wherefore, my brethren, ye also are become dead to the law by the body of Christ; that ye should be married to another, even to Him who is raised from the dead, that we should bring forth fruit unto God. [5] For when we were in the flesh, the motions of sins, which were by the law, did work in our members to bring forth fruit unto death. [6] But now we are delivered from the law, that being dead wherein we were held; that we should serve in newness of spirit, and not in the oldness of the letter. [7] What shall we say then? Is the law sin? God forbid. Nay, I had not known sin, but by the law: for I had not known lust, except the law had said, "Thou shalt not covet." (Romans 7:1-7)

21 I find then a law, that, when I would do good, evil is present with me. [22] For I delight in the law of God after the inward man: [23] But I see another law in my members, warring against the law of my mind, and bringing me into captivity to the law of sin which is in my members. [24] O wretched man that I am! Who shall deliver me from the body of this death? [25] I thank God through Jesus Christ our Lord. So then with the mind I myself serve the law of God; but with the flesh the law of sin. (Romans 7:21-25)

6

Christians
and the Law

Something in human nature makes us want to go to extremes, a weakness from which Christians are not wholly free. "Since we are saved by grace," some argue, "we are free to live as we please," which is the extreme of *license*.

"But we cannot ignore God's Law," others argue. "We are saved by grace, to be sure; but we must live under Law if we are to please God." This is the extreme expression of *legalism*.

Paul answered the first group in chapter 6; the second group he answered in chapter 7. The word *law* is used 23 times in this chapter. In chapter 6, Paul told us how to stop doing bad things; in chapter 7 he told how *not* to do good things. "You were not justified by keeping the Law," he argued, "and you cannot be sanctified by keeping the Law."

Every growing Christian understands the experience of Romans 6 and 7. Once we learn how to

"know, reckon, and yield," we start getting victory
over the habits of the flesh, and we feel we are
becoming more spiritual. We set high standards
and ideals for ourselves and for awhile seem to
attain them. *Then everything collapses!* We start
to see deeper into our own hearts and we discover
sins that we did not know were there. God's holy
Law takes on a new power, and we wonder if we
can ever do anything good! Without realizing it,
we have moved into "legalism" and have learned
the truth about sin, the Law, and ourselves.

What really is "legalism"? It is the belief that I
can become holy and please God by obeying laws.
It is measuring spirituality by a list of do's and
don'ts. The weakness of legalism is that it sees
sins (plural) but not *sin* (the root of the trouble).
It judges by the outward and not the inward.
Furthermore, the legalist fails to understand the
real purpose of God's Law and the relationship
between Law and grace.

In my pastoral experience, I have counseled
many people who have suffered severe emotional
and spiritual damage because they have tried to
live holy lives on the basis of a high standard. I
have seen the consequences of these attempts:
either the person becomes a pretender, or he suf-
fers a complete collapse and abandons his desires
for godly living. I have seen, too, that many legalists
are extremely hard on other people—critical, un-
loving, unforgiving. Paul wanted to spare his readers this difficult and dangerous experience. In Romans 7, he discussed three topics, which, if understood and applied, will deliver us from legalism.

1. The Authority of the Law (7:1-6)

These verses actually continue the discussion that

Paul began in Romans 6:15, answering the question, "Shall we sin because we are not under the law, but under grace?" He used the illustration of a master and servant to explain how the Christian should yield himself to God. In this passage he used the illustration of a husband and wife to show that the believer has a new relationship to the Law because of his union with Jesus Christ.

The illustration is a simple one, but it has a profound application. When a man and woman marry, they are united for life. Marriage is a physical union ("They two shall be one flesh" Gen. 2:24) and can only be broken by a physical cause. One such cause is *death*. (Matt. 5:31-34 and 19:1-12 indicate that unfaithfulness also breaks the marriage bond, but Paul does not bring this up. He is not discussing marriage and divorce; he is using marriage to illustrate a point.)

As long as they live, the husband and wife are under the authority of the law of marriage. If the woman leaves the man and marries another man, she commits adultery. But if the husband dies, she is free to remarry because she is no longer a wife. It is death that has broken the marriage relationship and set her free.

Paul's *application* in verses 4 through 6 clinches the argument. He states two marvelous facts that explain the believer's relationship to the Law.

a. *We died to the Law* (7:4)—It appears that Paul has confused his illustration, but he has not. When we were unsaved ("in the flesh . . ." verse 5), we were under the authority of God's Law. We were condemned by that Law. When we trusted Christ and were united to Him, *we died to the Law* just as we died to the flesh (Rom. 6:1-10). The Law did not die; *we* died.

But in Paul's illustration from marriage, it was the *husband* who died and the wife who married again. If you and I are represented by the wife, and the Law is represented by the husband, then the application does not follow the illustration. If the wife died in the illustration, the only way she could marry again would be to come back from the dead. But that is exactly what Paul wants to teach! When we trusted Christ, we died to the Law; but in Christ, we arose from the dead and now are "married" (united) to Christ to live a new kind of life!

The Law did not die, because God's Law still rules over men. We died to the Law, and it no longer has dominion over us. But we are not "lawless"; we are united to Christ, sharing His life, and thus walking "in newness of life." Romans 8:4 climaxes the argument: "That the righteousness of the law might be fulfilled in us, who walk not after the flesh but after the Spirit." In the old life of sin, we brought forth fruit "unto death", but in the new life of grace, we "bring forth fruit unto God." To be "dead to the law" does not mean that we lead lawless lives. It simply means that the *motivation* and *dynamic* of our lives does not come from the Law: it comes from God's grace through our union with Christ.

b. *We are delivered from Law* (7:6)—This is the logical conclusion: the Law cannot exercise authority over a dead person. The Authorized Version reads as though the Law died; but Paul wrote "we having died to that wherein we were held . . ." Death means deliverance (note Rom. 6:9-10). But we were delivered that we might serve. The Christian life is not one of independence and rebellion. We died to the Law that we might be "married to Christ." We were delivered from the Law that we might serve Christ. This truth refutes the false accusation that Paul taught lawlessness.

What is different about Christian service as opposed to our old life of sin? To begin with, the Holy Spirit of God energizes us as we seek to obey and serve the Lord. (The word spirit ought to be capitalized in verse 6—"newness of Spirit.") Under Law, no enablement was given. God's commandments were written on stones and read to the people. But under Grace, God's Word is written in our hearts (2 Cor. 3:1-3). We "walk in newness of life" (Rom. 6:4) and serve "in newness of Spirit." The believer, then, is no longer under the authority of the Law.

2. The Ministry of the Law (7:7-13)

Paul's objectors were ready! "What good is the Law if we don't need it any more? Why, a teaching such as yours turns the Law into sin!" In answering that objection, Paul explained the ministries of the Law, ministries that function even today.

a. *The Law reveals sin* (7:7)—"By the law is the knowledge of sin" (Rom. 3:20). "Where no law is, there is no transgression" (Rom. 4:15). The Law is a mirror that reveals to us the inner man and shows us how dirty we are (James 1:22-25). Note that Paul did not use murder, stealing, or adultery in his discussion; he uses *coveting*. This is the last of the Ten Commandments, and it differs from the other nine in that it is an inward attitude, not an outward action. Covetousness leads to the breaking of the other commandments! It is an insidious sin that most people never recognize in their own lives, but God's Law reveals it.

The Rich Ruler in Mark 10:17-27 is a good example of the use of the Law to reveal sin and show a man his need for a Saviour. The young man was very moral outwardly, but he had never faced the sins within. Jesus did not tell him about the Law because the Law would save him; He told him about the Law because the young man did not realize his own sinfulness. True, he had never committed adultery, robbed anyone, given false witness, or dishonored his parents; but what about covetousness? When Jesus told him to sell his goods and give to the poor, the man went away in great sorrow. The Commandment "Thou shalt not covet" had revealed to him what a sinner he really was! Instead of admitting his sin, he rejected Christ and went away unconverted.

b. *The Law arouses sin* (7:8-9)—Since Paul was a devout Pharisee, seeking to obey the Law before his conversion, it is easier to understand these verses. (Read Phil. 3:1-11 and Gal. 1 for other autobiographical data on Paul's relationship to the Law in his unconverted days.) Keep in mind, too, that "the strength of sin is the law" (1 Cor. 15:56). Since we have a sinful nature, the Law is bound to arouse that nature the way a magnet draws steel.

Something in human nature wants to rebel whenever a law is given. I was standing in Lincoln Park in Chicago, looking at the newly painted benches; and I noticed a sign on each bench: "Do Not Touch." As I watched, I saw numbers of people deliberately reach out and touch the wet paint! Why? Because the sign told them not to! Instruct a child not to go near the water, and that is the very thing he will do! Why? "Because the carnal mind is enmity against God: for it is not subject to the law of God, neither indeed can be" (Rom. 8:7).

Believers who try to live by rules and regulations discover that their legalistic system only arouses more sin and creates more problems. The churches in Galatia were very legalistic, and they experienced all kinds of trouble. "But if ye bite and devour one another, take heed that ye be not consumed one of another" (Gal. 5:15). Their legalism did not make them more spiritual; it made them more sinful! Why? Because the Law arouses sin in our nature.

c. *The Law kills* (7:10-11)—"For if there had been a law given which could have given life, verily righteousness should have been by the law" (Gal. 3:21). But the Law cannot give life: it can only show the sinner that he is guilty and condemned. This explains why legalistic Christians and churches do not grow and bear spiritual fruit. They are living by Law, and the Law always kills. Few things are more dead than an orthodox church that is proud of its "high standards" and tries to live up to them in its own energy. Often the members of such a church start to judge and condemn one another, and the sad result is a church fight and then a church split that leaves members— or former members—angry and bitter.

As the new Christian grows, he comes into contact with various philosophies of the Christian life. He can read books, attend seminars, listen to tapes, and get a great deal of information. If he is not careful, he will start following a human leader and accept his teachings as Law. This practice is a very subtle form of legalism, and it kills spiritual growth. No human teacher can take the place of Christ; no book can take the place of the Bible. Men can give us information, but only the Spirit can give us illumination and help us understand spiritual truths. The Spirit enlightens us and enables us; no human leader can do that.

d. *The Law shows the sinfulness of sin* (7:12-13) —Unsaved people know that there is such a thing as sin; but they do not realize the sinfulness of sin. Many Christians do not realize the true nature of sin. We excuse our sins with words like "mistakes" or "weaknesses"; but God condemns our sins and tries to get us to see that they are "exceedingly sinful." Until we realize how wicked sin really is, we will never want to oppose it and live in victory.

Paul's argument here is tremendous: (1) the Law is not sinful—it is holy, just, and good; (2) but the Law reveals sin, arouses sin, and then uses sin to slay us; if something as good as the Law accomplishes these results, then something is radically wrong somewhere; (3) conclusion: see how sinful sin is when it can use something good like the Law to produce such tragic results. Sin is indeed "exceedingly sinful." The problem is not with the Law; the problem is with my sinful nature. This prepares the way for the third topic in this chapter.

3. The Inability of the Law (7:14-25)

Having explained what the Law is supposed to do, Paul now explains what the Law cannot do.

a. *The Law cannot change you* (7:14)—The character of the Law is described in four words: holy, just, good, and spiritual. That the Law is holy and just, nobody can deny, because it came from a holy God who is perfectly just in all that He says and does. The Law is good. It reveals God's holiness to us and helps us to see our need for a Saviour.

What does it mean that the Law is "spiritual"? It means that the Law deals with the inner man, the spiritual part of man, as well as with the outer actions. In the original giving of the Law in Exodus, the emphasis was on the outward actions. But when Moses restated the Law in Deuteronomy, he emphasized the inner quality of the Law as it relates to man's heart. This spiritual emphasis is stated clearly in Deuteronomy 10:12-13. The repetition of the word "love" in Deuteronomy also shows that the deeper interpretation of the Law relates to the inner man (Deut. 4:37; 6:4-6; 10:12; 11:1; 30:6, 16, 20).

Our nature is carnal (fleshly); but the Law's nature is spiritual. This explains why the old nature responds as it does to the Law. It has well been said, "The old nature knows no Law, the new nature needs no Law." The Law cannot transform the old nature; it can only reveal how sinful that old nature is. The believer who tries to live under Law will only *activate* the old nature; he will not eradicate it.

b. *The Law cannot enable you to do good* (7: 15-21)—Three times in this passage Paul stated that sin dwells in us (vv. 14, 18, 20). He was referring, of course, to the old nature. It is also true that the Holy Spirit dwells in us; and in chapter 8, Paul explained how the Spirit of God enables us to live in victory, something the Law cannot help us do.

The many pronouns in this section indicate that the writer is having a problem with *self*. This is not to say that the Christian is a split personality, because he is not. Salvation makes a man whole. But it does indicate that the believer's mind, will, and body can be controlled either by the old nature or the new nature, either by the flesh or the Spirit. The statements here indicate that the believer has two serious problems: (1) he cannot do the good he wants to do, and (2) he does the evil that he does not want to do.

Does this mean that Paul could not stop himself from breaking God's Law, that he was a liar and thief and murderer? Of course not! Paul was saying that *of himself* he could not obey God's Law; and that even when he did, evil was still present with him. No matter what he did, his deeds were tainted by sin. Even after he had done his best, he had to admit that he was "an unprofitable servant" (Luke 17:10). "So I find this law at work: when I want to do good, evil is right there with me" (Rom. 7:21, NIV). This, of course, is a different problem from that in chapter 6. The problem there was "How can I stop doing bad things?" while the problem here is "How can I ever do anything good?"

The legalist says, "Obey the Law and you will do good and live a good life." But the Law only reveals and arouses sin, showing how sinful it is! It is impossible for me to obey the Law because I have a sinful nature that rebels against the Law. Even if I think I have done good, I know that evil is present. The Law is good, but by nature, I am bad! So, the legalist is wrong: the Law cannot enable us to do good.

c. *The Law cannot set you free* (7:21-24)—The believer has an old nature that wants to keep him in bondage; "I will get free from these old sins!" the Christian says to himself. "I determine here and now that I will not do this any longer." What happens? He exerts all his willpower and energy, and for a time succeeds; but then when he least expects it, he falls again. Why? Because he tried to overcome his old nature with Law, and the Law cannot deliver us from the old nature. When you move under the Law, you are only making the old nature stronger; because "the strength of sin is the law" (1 Cor. 15:56). Instead of being a dynamo that gives us power to overcome, the Law is a magnet that draws out of us all kinds of sin and corruption. The inward man may delight in the Law of God (Ps. 119:35), but the old nature delights in breaking the Law of God. No wonder the believer under Law becomes tired and discouraged, and eventually gives up! He is a captive, and his condition is "wretched." (The Greek word indicates a person who is exhausted after a battle.) What could be more wretched than exerting all your energy to try to live a good life, only to discover that the best you do is still not good enough!

Is there any deliverance? Of course! "I thank God that there is Someone who shall deliver me— Jesus Christ our Lord!" Because the believer is united to Christ, he is dead to the Law and no longer under its authority. But he is alive to God and able to draw upon the power of the Holy Spirit. The explanation of this victory is given in chapter 8.

The final sentence in the chapter does not teach that the believer lives a divided life: sinning with his flesh but serving God with his mind. This would mean that his body was being used in two different ways *at the same time*, and this is impossible. The believer realizes that there is a struggle within him between the flesh and the Spirit (Gal. 5:16-18), but he knows that one or the other must be in control.

By "the mind" Paul meant "the inward man" (v.

22) as opposed to "the flesh" (v. 18). He amplified this thought in Romans 8:5-8. The old nature cannot do anything good. Everything the Bible says about the old nature is negative: "no good thing" (Rom. 7:18); "the flesh profiteth nothing" (John 6:63); "no confidence in the flesh" (Phil. 3:3). If we depend on the energy of the flesh, we cannot serve God, please God, or do any good thing. But if we yield to the Holy Spirit, then we have the power needed to obey His will. The flesh will never serve the Law of God because the flesh is at war with God. But the Spirit can only obey the Law of God! Therefore, the secret of doing good is to yield to the Holy Spirit.

Paul hinted at this in the early verses of this chapter when he wrote ". . . that we should bring forth fruit unto God" (v. 4). Just as we are dead to the old nature, so we are dead to the Law. But we are united to Christ and alive in Christ, and therefore can bring forth fruit unto God. It is our union with Christ that enables us to serve God acceptably. "For it is God which worketh in you, both to will and to do of His good pleasure" (Phil. 2:13). That solved Paul's problem in Romans 7:18: "For to will is present with me; but how to perform that which is good I find not."

The old nature knows no law and the new nature needs no law. Legalism makes a believer wretched because it grieves the new nature and aggravates the old nature! The legalist becomes a Pharisee whose outward actions are acceptable, but whose inward attitudes are despicable. No wonder Jesus called them "whited sepulchres, which indeed appear beautiful outward, but are within full of dead men's bones, and of all uncleanness" (Matt. 23:27). How wretched can you get!

The best is yet to come! The next chapter explains the work of the Holy Spirit in overcoming the bad and producing the good.

Romans 8:1-39

There is therefore now no condemnation to them which are in Christ Jesus, who walk not after the flesh, but after the Spirit. ²For the law of the Spirit of life in Christ Jesus has made me free from the law of sin and death. ³For what the law could not do, in that it was weak through the flesh, God sending His own Son in the likeness of sinful flesh, and for sin, condemned sin in the flesh: ⁴That the righteousness of the law might be fulfilled in us, who walk not after the flesh, but after the Spirit.   (Romans 8:1-4)

11 But if the Spirit of Him that raised up Jesus from the dead dwell in you, He that raised up Christ from the dead shall also quicken your mortal bodies by His Spirit that dwelleth in you. ¹²Therefore, brethren, we are debtors, not to the flesh, to live after the flesh. ¹³For if ye live after the flesh, ye shall die: but if ye through the Spirit do mortify the deeds of the body, ye shall live. ¹⁴For as many as are led by the Spirit of God, they are the sons of God. ¹⁵For ye have not received the spirit of bondage again to fear; but ye have received the Spirit of adoption, whereby we cry, Abba, Father. ¹⁶The Spirit itself beareth witness with our spirit, that we are the children of God: ¹⁷and if children, then heirs; heirs of God, and joint-heirs with Christ: if so be that we suffer with Him, that we may be also glorified together.   (Romans 8:11-17)

38 For I am persuaded, that neither death, nor life, nor angels, nor principalities, nor powers, nor things present, nor things to come, ³⁹nor height, nor depth, nor any other creature, shall be able to separate us from the love of God, which is in Christ Jesus our Lord.   (Romans 8:38-39)

7

Freedom
and Fulfillment

On January 6, 1941, President Franklin Delano Roosevelt addressed Congress on the state of the war in Europe. Much of what he said that day has been forgotten. But at the close of his address, he said that he looked forward "to a world founded upon four essential human freedoms." He named them: freedom of speech, freedom of worship, freedom from want, and freedom from fear. These words are still remembered, even though their ideals have not yet been realized anywhere in the world.

Romans 8 is the Christian's "Declaration of Freedom", for in it Paul declares the four spiritual freedoms we enjoy because of our union with Jesus Christ. A study of this chapter shows the emphasis on the Holy Spirit, who is mentioned nineteen times. "Where the Spirit of the Lord is, there is liberty" (2 Cor. 3:17).

1. Freedom from Judgment—No Condemnation (8:1-4)

Romans 3:20 shows the "therefore" of condemnation; but Romans 8:1 gives the "therefore" of *no* condemnation—a tremendous truth and the conclusion of a marvelous argument. (The words "who walk not . . . etc" do not belong here according to the best manuscripts. There are no conditions for us to meet.) The basis for this wonderful assurance is the phrase "in Christ Jesus." In Adam, we were condemned. In Christ, there is no condemnation!

The verse does not say "no mistakes" or "no failures," or even "no sins." Christians *do* fail and make mistakes, and they do sin. Abraham lied about his wife; David committed adultery; Peter tried to kill a man with his sword. To be sure, they suffered consequences because of their sins, but they did not suffer condemnation.

The Law condemns; but the believer has a new relationship to the Law, and therefore he cannot be condemned. Paul made three statements about the believer and the Law, and together they add up to: *no condemnation.*

a. *The Law cannot claim you* (8:2)—You have been made free from the law of sin and death. You now have life in the Spirit. You have moved into a whole new sphere of life in Christ. "The law of sin and death" is what Paul described in Romans 7:7-25. "The law of the Spirit of life" is described in Romans 8. The Law no longer has any jurisdiction over you: you are dead to the Law (Rom. 7:4) and free from the Law (Rom. 8:2).

b. *The Law cannot condemn you* (8:3)—Why? Because Christ has already suffered that condemnation for you on the cross. The Law could not save; it can only condemn. But God sent His Son

to save us and do what the Law could not do.
Jesus did not come as an angel; He came as a man.
He did not come "in sinful flesh," for that would
have made Him a sinner. He came in *the likeness*
of sinful flesh, as a man. He bore our sins in His
body on the cross.

The "law of double jeopardy" states that a man
cannot be tried twice for the same crime. Since
Jesus Christ paid the penalty for your sins, and
since you are "in Christ," God will not condemn
you.

c. *The Law cannot control you* (8:4)—The believer lives a righteous life, not in the power of the
Law, but in the power of the Holy Spirit. The Law
does not have the power to produce holiness; it can
only reveal and condemn sin. But the indwelling
Holy Spirit enables you to walk in obedience to
God's will. The righteousness that God demands in
His Law is fulfilled in you through the Spirit's
power. In the Holy Spirit, you have life and
liberty (Rom. 8:2) and "the pursuit of happiness"
(Rom. 8:4).

The legalist tries to obey God in his own strength
and fails to measure up to the righteousness that
God demands. The Spirit-led Christian, as he yields
to the Lord, experiences the sanctifying work of
the Spirit in his life. "For it is God that worketh in
you, both to will and to do of His good pleasure"
(Phil. 2:13). It is this fact that leads to the second
freedom we enjoy as Christians.

2. Freedom from Defeat—No Obligation (8:5-17)

"Therefore, brethren, we are debtors, not to the
flesh, to live after the flesh" (Rom. 8:12). There is
no obligation to the old nature. The believer can
live in victory. In this section, Paul described life on

three different levels; and he encouraged his readers to live on the highest level.

a. *"You have not the Spirit"* (8:5-8)—Paul is not describing two kinds of Christians, one carnal and one spiritual. He is contrasting the saved and the unsaved. There are four contrasts.

1. *In the flesh—In the Spirit* (8:5). The unsaved person does not have the Spirit of God (Rom. 8:9) and lives *in* the flesh and *for* the flesh. His mind is centered on the things that satisfy the flesh. But the Christian has the Spirit of God within and lives in an entirely new and different sphere. His mind is fixed on the things of the Spirit. This does not mean that the unsaved person never does anything good, or that the believer never does anything bad. It means that the bent of their lives is different. One lives for the flesh, the other lives for the Spirit.

2. *Death—Life* (8:6). The unsaved person is alive physically, but dead spiritually. The inner man is dead toward God and does not respond to the things of the Spirit. He may be moral, and even religious; but he lacks spiritual life. He needs "the Spirit of life in Christ Jesus . . ." (Rom. 8:2).

3. *War with God—peace with God* (8:6-7). In our study of Romans 7, we have seen that the old nature rebels against God and will not submit to God's Law. Those who have trusted Christ enjoy "peace with God" (Rom. 5:1), while the unsaved are at war with God. "There is no peace, saith the Lord, unto the wicked" (Isa. 48:22).

4. *Pleasing self—pleasing God* (8:8). To be "in the flesh" means to be lost, outside Christ. The unsaved person lives to please himself and rarely if ever thinks about pleasing God. The root of sin is selfishness—"I will" and not "Thy will."

To be unsaved and not have the Spirit is the lowest level of life. But a person need not stay on that level. By faith in Christ he can move to the second level.

b. *"You have the Spirit"* (8:9-11)—"But ye are not in the flesh, but in the Spirit, if so be that the Spirit of God dwell in you" (Rom. 8:9). The evidence of conversion is the presence of the Holy Spirit within, witnessing that you are a child of God (Rom. 8:16). Your body becomes the very temple of the Holy Spirit (1 Cor. 6:19-20). Even though the body is destined to die because of sin (unless, of course, the Lord returns), the Spirit gives life to that body today so that we may serve God. If we should die, the body will one day be raised from the dead, because the Holy Spirit has sealed each believer (Eph. 1:13-14).

What a difference it makes in your body when the Holy Spirit lives within. You experience new life, and even your physical faculties take on a new dimension of experience. When evangelist D. L. Moody described his conversion experience, he said: "I was in a new world. The next morning the sun shone brighter and the birds sang sweeter . . . the old elms waved their branches for joy, and all nature was at peace." Life in Christ is abundant life.

But there is a third level of experience for which the other two are preparation.

c. *"The Spirit has you!"* (Rom. 8:12-17)—It is not enough for us to have the Spirit; the Spirit must have us! Only then can He share with us the abundant, victorious life that can be ours in Christ. We have no obligation to the flesh, because the flesh has only brought trouble into our lives. We do have an obligation to the Holy Spirit, for it is the Spirit who convicted us, revealed Christ to us, and imparted eternal life to us when we trusted Christ. Because He is "the Spirit of Life," He can empower us to obey Christ, and He can enable us to be more like Christ.

But He is also the Spirit of death. He can enable us to "put to death" (mortify) the sinful deeds of the body. As we yield the members of our body to the Spirit (Rom. 6:12-17), He applies to us and in us the death and resurrection of Christ. He puts to death the things of the flesh, and He reproduces the things of the Spirit.

The Holy Spirit is also "the Spirit of adoption" (8:14-17). The word *adoption* in the New Testament means "being placed as an adult son." We come into God's family by birth. But the instant we are born into the family, God adopts us and gives us the position of an adult son. A baby cannot walk, speak, make decisions, or draw upon the family wealth. But the believer can do all of these the instant he is born again.

He can walk and be "led of the Spirit" (8:14). The verb here means "willingly led." We yield to the Spirit, and He guides us by His Word day by day. We are not under bondage to Law and afraid to act. We have the liberty of the Spirit and are free to follow Christ. The believer can also speak: "We cry, Abba, Father" (8:15). Would it not be amazing if a newborn baby looked up and greeted his father! First, the Spirit says "Abba, Father" to us (Gal. 4:6), and then we say it to God. ("Abba" means "papa"—a term of endearment.)

A baby cannot sign checks, but the child of God by faith can draw upon his spiritual wealth because he is an heir of God and a joint-heir with Christ (8:17). The Spirit teaches us from the Word, and then we receive God's wealth by faith. What a thrilling thing it is to have "the Spirit of adoption" at work in our lives!

There is no need for the believer to be defeated. He can yield his body to the Spirit and by faith overcome the old nature. The Spirit of life will empower him. The Spirit of death will enable him to overcome the flesh. And the Spirit of adoption will enrich him and lead him into the will of God.

3. Freedom from Discouragement—No Frustration (8:18-30)

Paul in this section dealt with the very real problem of suffering and pain. Perhaps the best way to understand this section is to note the three "groans" that are discussed.

a. *Creation groans* (8:18-22)—When God finished His creation, it was a good creation (Genesis 1:31); but today it is a groaning creation. There is suffering and death; there is pain, all of which is, of course, the result of Adam's sin. It is not the fault of creation. Note the words that Paul used to describe the plight of creation: suffering (v. 18), vanity (v. 20), bondage (v. 21), decay (v. 21), and pain (v. 22). However, this groaning is not a useless thing: Paul compared it to a woman in travail. There is pain, but the pain will end when the child is delivered. One day creation will be delivered, and the groaning creation will become a glorious creation! The believer does not focus on today's sufferings; he looks forward to tomorrow's glory (v. 18; 2 Cor. 4:15-18). Today's groaning bondage will be exchanged for tomorrow's glorious liberty!

b. *We believers groan* (8:23-25)—The reason we groan is because we have experienced "the firstfruits of the Spirit," a foretaste of the glory to come. Just as the nation of Israel tasted the firstfruits of Canaan when the spies returned (Num. 13:23-27), so we Christians have tasted of the blessings of heaven through the ministry of the Spirit. This makes us want to see the Lord, receive a new body, and live with Him and serve Him forever. We are waiting for "the adoption," which is the redemption of the body when Christ returns (Phil. 3:20-21). This is the thrilling climax to "the adoption" that took place at conversion when "the Spirit of adoption" gave us an adult standing in God's family. When Christ returns, we shall enter into our full inheritance.

Meanwhile, we wait and hope. "For we are saved by that hope" (8:24, literal translation). What hope? "That blessed hope and the glorious appearing of the great God and our Saviour Jesus Christ" (Titus 2:13). The best is yet to come! The believer does not get frustrated as he sees and experiences suffering and pain in this world. He knows that the temporary suffering will one day give way to eternal glory.

c. *The Holy Spirit groans* (8:25-30)—God is concerned about the trials of His people. When He was ministering on earth, Jesus groaned when He saw what sin was doing to mankind (Mark 7:34; John 11:33, 38). Today the Holy Spirit groans with us and feels the burdens of our weaknesses and suffering. But the Spirit does more than groan. He prays for us in His groaning so that we might be led into the will of God. We do not always know God's will. We do not always know how to pray, but the Spirit intercedes so that we might live in the will of God in spite of suffering. The Spirit "shares the burden."

The believer never need faint in times of suffering and trial because he knows that God is at work in the world (8:28), and that He has a perfect plan (8:29). God has two purposes in that plan: our good and His glory. Ultimately, He will make us like Jesus Christ! Best of all, God's plan is going to succeed! It started in eternity past when He chose us in Christ (Eph. 1:4-5). He predetermined that one day we would be like His Son. Predestination applies only to saved people. Nowhere are we taught that God predestines people to be eternally condemned. If they are condemned, it is because of their refusal to trust Christ (John 3:18-21). Those whom He chose, He called (see 2 Thes. 2:13-14); when they responded to His call, He justified them, and He also glorified them. This means that the believer has already been glorified in Christ (John 17:22); the revelation of this glory awaits the coming of the Lord (Rom. 8:21-23).

How can we Christians ever be discouraged and frustrated when we already share the glory of God? Our suffering today only guarantees that much more glory when Jesus Christ returns!

4. Freedom from Fear—No Separation (8:31-39)

There is no condemnation because we share the righteousness of God and the Law cannot condemn us. There is no obligation because we have the Spirit of God who enables us to overcome the flesh and live for God. There is no frustration because we share the glory of God, the blessed hope of Christ's return. There is no separation because we experience the love of God: "What shall separate us from the love of Christ?" (Rom. 8:35). The emphasis in this final section is on the security of the believer. We do not need to fear the past, present, or future because we are secure in the love of Christ. Paul presented five arguments to prove that there could be no separation between the believer and the Lord.

a. *God is for us* (8:31)—*The Father* is for us and proved it by giving His Son (8:32). *The Son* is for us (8:34) and so is *the Spirit* (8:26). God is making all things work for us (8:28). In His Person and His providence, God is for us. Sometimes, like Jacob, we lament, "All these things are against me," (Gen. 42:36), when actually everything is working for us. The conclusion is obvious: "If God be for us, who can be against us?"

The believer needs to enter into each new day realizing that God is for him. There is no need to fear, for his loving Father desires only the best for His children, even if they must go through trials to receive His best. "For I know the plans that I have for you, declares the Lord, plans for welfare and not for calamity to give you a future and a hope" (Jer. 29:11, NASB).

b. *Christ died for us* (8:32)—The argument here is from the lesser to the greater. If when we were sinners, God gave us His best, now that we are God's children, will He not give us all that we need? Jesus used this same argument when He tried to convince people that it was foolish to worry and fear. God cares for the birds and sheep, and even for the lilies; surely He will care for you! God is dealing with His own on the basis of Calvary grace, not on the basis of Law. God freely gives all things to His own!

c. *God has justified us* (8:33)—This means that He has declared us righteous in Christ. Satan would like to accuse us (Rev. 12:10; Zech. 3:1-7),

but we stand righteous in Jesus Christ. We are
God's elect—chosen in Christ and accepted in
Christ. God will certainly not accuse us since it is
He who has justified us. For Him to accuse us
would mean that His salvation was a failure and
we are still in our sins.

Understanding the meaning of justification
brings peace to our hearts. When God declares the
believing sinner righteous in Christ, that declaration never changes. Our Christian experience
changes from day to day, but justification never
changes. We may accuse ourselves, and men may
accuse us; but God will never take us to court and
accuse us. Jesus has already paid the penalty and
we are secure in Him.

d. *Christ intercedes for us* (8:34)—A dual intercession keeps the believer secure in Christ: the
Spirit intercedes (8:26-27) and the Son of God
intercedes (8:34). The same Saviour who died for
us is now interceding for us in heaven. As our High
Priest, He can give us the grace we need to overcome temptation and defeat the enemy (Heb.
4:14-16). As our Advocate, He can forgive our sins
and restore our fellowship with God (1 John 1:9—
2:2). Intercession means that Jesus Christ repre-
sents us before the throne of God and we do not
have to represent ourselves.

Paul hinted at this ministry of intercession in
Romans 5:9-10. We are not only saved by His
death, but we are also saved by His life. "Therefore He is able to save completely those who come
to God through Him, because He always lives to
intercede for them" (Heb. 7:25, NIV). Peter sinned
against the Lord, but he was forgiven and restored
to fellowship because of Jesus Christ. "Simon, Simon, listen! Satan has asked permission to sift all

of you like wheat, but I have prayed especially for you that your own faith may not utterly fail" (Luke 22:31-32, wms). He is interceding for each of us, a ministry that assures us that we are secure.

e. *Christ loves us* (8:35-39)—In verses 31-34 Paul has proved that God cannot fail us, but is it possible that we can fail Him? Suppose some great trial or temptation comes, and we fail? Then what? Paul deals with that problem in this final section and explains that nothing can separate us from the love of Jesus Christ.

To begin with, God does not shelter us from the difficulties of life because we need them for our spiritual growth (Rom. 5:3-5). In Romans 8:28 God assures us that the difficulties of life are working *for* us and not *against* us. God permits trials to come that we might use them for our good and His glory. We endure trials for His sake (8:36), and since we do, do you think that He will desert us? Of course not! Instead, He is closer to us when we go through the difficulties of life.

Furthermore, He gives us the power to conquer (v. 37). We are "more than conquerors," literally, "we are superconquerors" through Jesus Christ! He gives us victory and more victory! We need not fear life or death, things present or things to come, because Jesus Christ loves us and gives us the victory. This is not a promise with conditions attached: "If you do this, God will do that." This security in Christ is an established fact, and we claim it for ourselves because we are in Christ. Nothing can separate you from His love! Believe it—and rejoice in it!

A review of this wonderful chapter shows that the Christian is completely victorious. We are free from judgment because Christ died for us and we have His righteousness. We are free from defeat because Christ lives in us by His Spirit and we share His life. We are free from discouragement because Christ is coming for us and we shall share His glory. We are free from fear because Christ intercedes for us and we cannot be separated from His love.

No condemnation! No obligation! No frustration! No separation!

If God be for us, who can be against us!

I say the truth in Christ, I lie not, my conscience also bearing me witness in the Holy Ghost, ² That I have great heaviness and continual sorrow in my heart. ³ For I could wish that myself were accursed from Christ for my brethren, my kinsmen according to the flesh: ⁴ Who are Israelites; to whom pertaineth the adoption, and the glory, and the covenants, and the giving of the law, and the service of God, and the promises; ⁵ Whose are the fathers, and of whom as concerning the flesh Christ came, who is over all, God blessed forever. Amen. (Romans 9:1-5)

20 Nay but, O man, who art thou that repliest against God? Shall the thing formed say to him that formed it, "Why hast thou made me thus?" ²¹ Hath not the potter power over the clay, of the same lump to make one vessel unto honour, and another unto dishonour? ²² What if God, willing to show His wrath, and to make His power known, endured with much longsuffering the vessels of wrath fitted to destruction: ²³ And that He might make known the riches of His glory on the vessels of mercy, which He had afore prepared unto glory, ²⁴ Even us, whom He hath called, not of the Jews only, but also of the Gentiles? (Romans 9:20-24)

30 What shall we say then? That the Gentiles, which followed not after righteousness, have attained to righteousness, even the righteousness which is of faith. ³¹ But Israel, which followed after the law of righteousness, hath not attained to the law of righteousness. ³² Wherefore? Because they sought it not by faith, but as it were by the works of the law. For they stumbled at that stumblingstone; ³³ As it is written, "Behold I lay in Sion a stumblingstone and rock of offence: and whosoever believeth on Him shall not be ashamed." (Romans 9:30-33)

8

Did God Make
a Mistake?

It seems strange that Paul would interrupt his discussion of salvation and devote a long section of three chapters to the nation of Israel. Why didn't he move from the doctrinal teaching of chapter 8 to the practical duties given in 12—15? A careful study of Romans 9—11 reveals that this section is not an interruption at all; it is a necessary part of Paul's argument for justification by faith.

To begin with, Paul was considered a traitor to the Jewish nation. He ministered to Gentiles and he taught freedom from the Law of Moses. He had preached in many synagogues and caused trouble, and no doubt many of the Jewish believers in Rome had heard of his questionable reputation. In these chapters, Paul showed his love for Israel and his desire for their welfare. This is the personal reason for this discussion.

But there was a doctrinal reason. Paul had

argued in Romans 8 that the believer is secure in Jesus Christ and that God's election would stand (8:28-30). But someone might ask, "What about the Jews? They were chosen by God, and yet now you tell us they are set aside and God is building His Church. Did God fail to keep His promises to Israel?" In other words, the very character of God was at stake. If God was not faithful to the Jews, how do we know He will be faithful to the Church?

The emphasis in chapter 9 is on Israel's past election, in chapter 10 on Israel's present rejection, and in chapter 11 on Israel's future restoration. Israel is the only nation in the world with a complete history—past, present, and future. In chapter 9, Paul defended the character of God by showing that Israel's past history actually magnified the attributes of God. He specifically named four attributes of God: His faithfulness (vv. 1-13), righteousness (vv. 14-18), justice (vv. 19-29), and grace (vv. 30-33). You will note that these divisions correspond with Paul's three questions: "Is there unrighteousness with God?" (v. 14); "Why doth He find fault?" (v. 19); and "What shall we say then?" (v. 30)

1. God's Faithfulness (9:1-13)

It is remarkable how Paul moved from the joy of chapter 8 into the sorrow and burden of chapter 9. When he looked at Christ, he rejoiced; but when he looked at the lost people of Israel, he wept. Like Moses (Ex. 32:30-35), he was willing to be cursed and separated from Christ if it would mean the salvation of Israel. What a man this Paul was! He was willing to stay out of heaven for the sake of the saved (9:3), and willing to go to hell for the sake of the lost.

His theme was God's election of Israel; and the first thing he dealt with was the blessing of their election (vv. 4-5). Israel was adopted by God as His own people (Ex. 4:22-23). He gave them His glory in the tabernacle and the temple (Ex. 40:34-38; 1 Kings 8:10-11). The glory Moses beheld on Mount Sinai came to dwell with Israel (Ex. 24:16-17). God gave Israel His covenants, the first to Abraham, and then additional covenants to Moses and to David. He also gave them His Law to govern their political, social, and religious life, and to guarantee His blessing if they obeyed. He gave them "the service of God," referring to the ministry in the tabernacle and the temple. He gave them the promises and the patriarchs ("the fathers" in verse 5). The purpose of all of this blessing was that Jesus Christ, through Israel, might come into the world. (Note that verse 5 affirms that Jesus Christ is God.) All of these blessings were given freely to Israel and to no other nation.

But in spite of these blessings, Israel failed. When the Messiah appeared, Israel rejected Him and crucified Him. No one knew this better than Paul, because in his early days he had persecuted the Church. Does Israel's failure mean that God's Word has failed? (The Greek word translated "taken none effect" pictures a ship going off its course.) The answer is, "No! God is faithful no matter what men may do with His Word." Here Paul explains the basis for Israel's election.

a. *It was not of natural descent* (9:6-10)—As we saw in Romans 2:25-29, there is a difference between the natural seed of/ Abraham and the spiritual children of Abraham. Abraham actually had two sons, Ishmael (by Hagar) and Isaac (by Sarah). Since Ishmael was the firstborn, he should

have been chosen, but it was Isaac that God
chose. Isaac and Rebecca had twin sons, Esau and
Jacob. As the firstborn, Esau should have been
chosen, but it was Jacob that God chose. And Esau
and Jacob had the same father and mother, unlike
Ishmael and Isaac who had the same father but
different mothers. God did not base His election
on the physical. Therefore, if the nation of Israel—
Abraham's physical descendants—has rejected
God's Word, this does not nullify God's elective
purposes at all.

b. *It is not of human merit* (9:11-13)—God chose
Jacob before the babies were born. The two boys
had done neither good nor evil, so God's choice
was not based on their character or conduct. Verse
13 is a reference to Malachi 1:2-3 and refers to
nations (Israel and Edom) and not individual sinners. God does not hate sinners. John 3:16 makes it
clear that He loves sinners. The statement here has
to do with national election, not individual. Since
God's election of Israel does not depend on human
merit, their disobedience cannot nullify the elective purposes of God. God is faithful even though
His people are unfaithful.

2. God's Righteousness (9:14-18)

The fact that God chose one and not the other
seems to indicate that He is unrighteous. "Is there
unrighteousness with God?" Paul asked; and then
he replied, "God forbid!" It is unthinkable that a
holy God should ever commit an unrighteous act.
Election is always totally a matter of grace. If God
acted only on the basis of righteousness, nobody
would ever be saved. Paul quoted Exodus 33:19
to show that God's mercy and compassion are
extended according to God's will and not man's

will. All of us deserve condemnation—not mercy.
The reference in Exodus 33 deals with Israel's
idolatry while Moses was on the mount receiving
the Law. The whole nation deserved to be destroyed, yet God killed only 3,000 people—not because the others were more wicked or less godly,
but purely because of His grace and mercy.

Paul then quoted Exodus 9:16, using Pharaoh as
an illustration. Moses was a Jew, Pharaoh was a
Gentile; yet both were sinners. In fact, both were
murderers! Both saw God's wonders. Yet Moses
was saved and Pharaoh was lost. God raised up
Pharaoh that He might reveal His glory and power;
and He had mercy on Moses that He might use him
to deliver the people of Israel. Pharaoh was a ruler,
and Moses was a slave; yet it was Moses who
experienced the mercy and compassion of God—
because God willed it that way. God is sovereign
in His work and acts according to His own will and
purposes. So it was not a matter of righteousness
but of the sovereign will of God.

God is holy and must punish sin; but God is
loving and desires to save sinners. If everybody is
saved, it would deny His holiness; but if everybody is lost, it would deny His love. The solution
to the problem is God's sovereign election.

A seminary professor once said to me, "Try to
explain election, and you may lose your mind; but
explain it away and you will lose your soul!"

God chose Israel and condemned Egypt, because this was His sovereign purpose. Nobody
can condemn God for the way He extends His
mercy, because God is righteous.

Before leaving this section, we need to discuss
the "hardening" of Pharaoh (v. 18). This hardening process is referred to at least 15 times in

Exodus 7—14. Sometimes we are told that Pharaoh hardened his heart (Ex. 8:15, 19, 32), and other times that God hardened Pharaoh's heart (Ex. 9:12; 10:1, 20, 27). By declaring His Word and revealing His power, God gave Pharaoh opportunity to repent; but instead, Pharaoh resisted God and hardened his heart. The fault lay not with God but Pharaoh. The same sunlight that melts the ice also hardens the clay. God was not unrighteous in His dealings with Pharaoh because He gave him many opportunities to repent and believe.

3. God's Justice (9:19-29)

But this fact of God's sovereign will only seems to create a new problem. "If God is sovereign, then who can resist Him? And if one does resist Him, what right does He have to judge?" It is the age-old question of the justice of God as He works in human history.

I recall sharing in a street meeting in Chicago and passing out tracts at the corner of Madison and Kedzie. Most of the people graciously accepted the tracts, but one man took the tract and with a snarl crumpled it up and threw it in the gutter. The name of the tract was "Four Things God Wants You To Know."

"There are a few things I would like God to know!" the man said. "Why is there so much sorrow and tragedy in this world? Why do the innocent suffer while the rich go free? Bah! Don't tell me there's a God! If there is, then God is the biggest sinner that ever lived!" And he turned away with a sneer and was lost in the crowd.

We know that God by nature is perfectly just. "Shall not the Judge of all the earth do right?" (Gen. 18:25). It is unthinkable that God would will an unjust purpose or perform an unjust act. But at times it seems that He does just that. He had mercy on Moses but condemned Pharaoh. Is this just? He elected Israel and rejected the other nations. Is this just? Paul gives three answers to this charge.

a. *Who are we to argue with God?* (9:19-21)— This is a logical argument. God is the potter and we are the clay. God is wiser than we are and we are foolish to question His will or to resist it. (The reference here is to Isa. 45:9.) To be sure, the clay has no life and is passive in the potter's hand. We have feelings, intellect, and willpower, and we can resist Him if we choose. (See Jeremiah 18 where this thought is developed.) But it is God who determines whether a man will be a Moses or a Pharaoh. Neither Moses, nor Pharaoh, nor anyone else, could choose his parents, his genetic structure, or his time and place of birth. We have to believe that these matters are in the hands of God.

However, this does not excuse us from responsibility. Pharaoh had great opportunities to learn about the true God and trust Him, and yet he chose to rebel. Paul did not develop this aspect of truth because his theme was divine sovereignty, not human responsibility. The one does not deny the other, even though our finite minds may not fully grasp them both.

b. *God has His purposes* (9:22-24)—We must never think that God enjoyed watching a tyrant like Pharaoh. He endured it. God said to Moses, "I have surely seen the affliction of my people . . . and have heard their cry . . . for I know their sorrows" (Ex. 3:7). The fact that God was longsuffering indicates that He gave Pharaoh opportunities to be saved (see 2 Peter 3:9). The word "fitted" in verse 22 does not suggest that *God* made Pharaoh a "vessel of wrath." The verb is in what the Greek grammarians call the middle voice, making it a reflexive action verb. So, it should read: *"fitted himself* for destruction." God prepares men for glory (v. 23), but sinners prepare themselves for judgment. In Moses and Israel God revealed the riches of His mercy; in Pharaoh and Egypt He revealed His power and wrath. Since neither deserved any mercy, God cannot be charged with injustice.

Ultimately, of course, God's purpose was to form His Church from both Jews and Gentiles (v. 24). Believers today are, by God's grace, "vessels of mercy" which He is preparing for glory, a truth that reminds us of Romans 8:29-30.

c. *All of this was prophesied* (9:25-29)—First Paul quoted Hosea 2:23, a statement declaring that God would turn from the Jews and call the Gentiles. Then he cited Hosea 1:10 to prove that this new people being called would be God's people and "children of the living God." He then quoted Isaiah 10:22-23 to show that only a remnant of Israel would be saved, while the greater part of the nation would suffer judgment. Verse 28 probably refers to God's work of judgment during the Tribulation, when the nation of Israel will be persecuted and judged, and only a small remnant left to enter into the kingdom when Jesus Christ returns to earth. But the application for today is clear: only a remnant of Jews are believing; and they, together with the Gentiles, are the "called of God" (v. 24). The final quotation from Isaiah 1:9 emphasized the grace of God in sparing the believing remnant.

Now, what does all of this prove? That God was not unjust in saving some and judging others, because He was only fulfilling the Old Testament prophecies given centuries ago. He would be unjust if He did not keep His own Word. But even more than that, these prophecies show that God's election has made possible the salvation of the Gentiles. This is the grace of God. At the exodus, God rejected the Gentiles and chose the Jews, so that, through the Jews, He might save the Gentiles. The nation of Israel rejected His will, but this did not defeat His purposes. A remnant of Jews does believe and God's Word has been fulfilled.

So far, Paul had defended the character of God by showing His faithfulness, His righteousness, and His justice. Israel's rejection had not canceled God's election; it had only proved that He was true to His character and His purposes.

4. God's Grace (9:30-33)

Paul moved next from divine sovereignty to human responsibility. Note that Paul did not say "elect" and "nonelect," but rather emphasized faith. Here is a paradox: the Jews sought for righteousness but did not find it, while the Gentiles, who were not searching for it, found it! The reason? Israel tried to be saved by works and not by faith. They rejected "grace righteousness" and tried to please God with "Law righteousness." The Jews thought that the Gentiles had to *come up* to Israel's level to be saved; when actually the Jews had to *go down* to the level of the Gentiles to be saved. "For there is no difference: for all have sinned and come short of the glory of God" (Rom. 3:22-23). Instead of permitting their religious privileges (Rom. 9:1-5) to lead them to Christ, they used these privileges as a substitute for Christ.

But see the grace of God: Israel's rejection means

the Gentiles' salvation! Paul's final quotation was from Isaiah 28:16. It referred to Christ, God's Stone of salvation. (See Ps. 118:22.) God gave Christ to be a Foundation Stone, but Israel rejected Him and He became a stumbling stone. Instead of "rising" on this Stone, Israel fell (Rom. 11:11); but, as we shall see, their fall made possible the salvation of the Gentiles by the grace of God.

We need to decide what kind of righteousness we are seeking, whether we are depending on good works and character, or trusting Christ alone for salvation. God does not save people on the basis of birth or behavior. He saves them "by grace, through faith" (Eph. 2:8-9). It is not a question of whether or not we are among God's elect. That is a mystery known only to God. He offers us His salvation by faith. The offer is made to "whosoever will" (Rev. 22:17). After we have trusted Christ, then we have the witness and evidence that we are among His elect (Eph. 1:4-14; 1 Thes. 1:1-10). But first we must trust Him and receive by faith His righteousness which alone can guarantee heaven.

No one will deny that there are many mysteries connected with divine sovereignty and human responsibility. Nowhere does God ask us to choose between these two truths, because they both come from God and are a part of God's plan. They do not compete; they cooperate. The fact that we cannot fully understand *how* they work together does not deny the fact that they do. When a man asked Charles Spurgeon how he reconciled divine sovereignty and human responsibility, Spurgeon replied: "I never try to reconcile friends!"

But the main thrust of this chapter is clear: Israel's rejection of Christ does not deny the faithfulness of God. Romans 9 does not negate Romans

8. God is still faithful, righteous, just, and gracious, and He can be depended upon to accomplish His purposes and keep His promises.

Romans 10:1-21

Brethren, my heart's desire and prayer to God for Israel is that they might be saved. ² For I bear them record that they have a zeal of God, but not according to knowledge. ³ For they being ignorant of God's righteousness, and going about to establish their own righteousness, have not submitted themselves unto the righteousness of God. ⁴ For Christ is the end of the law for righteousness to every one that believeth. ⁵ For Moses describeth the righteousness which is of the law, That the man which doeth those things shall live by them. (Romans 10:1-5)

9 That if thou shalt confess with thy mouth the Lord Jesus, and shalt believe in thine heart that God hath raised Him from the dead, thou shalt be saved. ¹⁰ For with the heart man believeth unto righteousness; and with the mouth confession is made unto salvation. ¹¹ For the Scripture saith, "Whosoever believeth on Him shall not be ashamed. ¹² For there is no difference between the Jew and the Greek: for the same Lord over all is rich unto all that call upon Him. ¹³ For whosoever shall call upon the name of the Lord shall be saved. ¹⁴ How then shall they call on Him in whom they have not believed? And how shall they believe in Him of whom they have not heard? And how shall they hear without a preacher? ¹⁵ And how shall they preach except they be sent? As it is written, "How beautiful are the feet of them that preach the Gospel of peace, and bring glad tidings of good things!" (Romans 10:9-15)

9

The Wrong Righteousness

The theme of this chapter is Israel's present rejection. Paul moved from divine sovereignty (chapter 9) to human responsibility. He continued the theme of righteousness introduced at the end of the previous chapter (9:30-33) and explains three aspects of Israel's rejection.

1. The Reasons for Their Rejection (10:1-13)

You would think that Israel as a nation would have been eagerly expecting the arrival of their Messiah and been prepared to receive Him. For centuries they had known the Old Testament prophecies and had practiced the Law, which was "a schoolmaster" to lead them to Christ (Gal. 3:24). God had sought to prepare the nation, but when Jesus Christ came, they rejected Him. "He came unto His own [world] and His own [people] received Him not" (John 1:11). To be sure, there was a faithful remnant in the nation that looked for His arrival, such as Simeon and Anna (Luke 2:25-38); but the majority of the people were not ready when He came.

How do we explain this tragic event? Paul gives several reasons why Israel rejected their Messiah.

a. *They did not feel a need for salvation* (10:1) —There was a time when Paul would have agreed with his people, for he himself opposed the Gospel and considered Jesus Christ an imposter. Israel considered the Gentiles in need of salvation, but certainly not the Jews. In several of His parables, Jesus pointed out this wrong attitude: the Elder Brother (Luke 15:11-32) and the Pharisee (Luke 18:9-14) are two examples. Israel would have been happy for political salvation from Rome, but she did not feel she needed spiritual salvation from her own sin.

b. *They were zealous for God* (10:2)—Ever since Israel returned to their land from Babylonian captivity, the nation had been cured of idolatry. In the temple and the local synagogues, only the true God was worshiped and served, and only the true Law was taught. So zealous were the Jews that they even "improved upon God's Law" and added their own traditions, making them equal to the Law. Paul himself had been zealous for the Law and the traditions (Acts 26:1-11; Gal. 1:13-14).

But their zeal was not based on knowledge; it was heat without light. Sad to say, many religious people today are making the same mistake. They think that their good works and religious deeds will save them, when actually these practices are keeping them from being saved. Certainly many of them are sincere and devout, but sincerity and devotion will never save the soul. "Therefore by the deeds of the law there shall no flesh be justified in His sight" (Rom. 3:20).

c. *They were proud and self-righteous* (10:3)— Israel was ignorant of God's righteousness, not because they had never been told, but because they refused to learn. There is an ignorance that comes from lack of opportunity, but Israel had had many opportunities to be saved. In their case, it was an ignorance that stemmed from wilful, stubborn resistance to the truth. They would not submit to God. They were proud of their own good works and religious self-righteousness, and would not admit their sins and trust the Saviour. Paul had made the same mistake before he met the Lord (Phil. 3:1-11).

The godly Presbyterian preacher, Robert Murray McCheyne, was passing out tracts one day and handed one to a well-dressed lady. She gave him a haughty look and said, "Sir, you must not know who I am!"

In his kind way, McCheyne replied, "Madam, there is coming a day of judgment, and on that day it will not make any difference who you are!"

d. *They misunderstood their own Law* (10:4-13) —Everything about the Jewish religion pointed to the coming Messiah—their sacrifices, priesthood, temple services, religious festivals, and covenants. Their Law told them they were sinners in need of a Saviour. But instead of letting the Law bring them to Christ (Gal. 3:24), they worshiped their Law and rejected their Saviour. The Law was a signpost, pointing the way. But it could never take them to their destination. The Law cannot give righteousness; it only leads the sinner to the Saviour who can give righteousness.

Christ is "the end of the law" in the sense that

through His death and resurrection, He has terminated the ministry of the Law for those who believe. The Law is ended as far as Christians are concerned. The righteousness of the Law is being fulfilled in the life of the believer through the power of the Spirit (Rom. 8:4); but the reign of the Law has ended. (See Eph. 2:15 and Col. 2:14.) "For ye are not under the law, but under grace" (Rom. 6:14).

Paul quoted from the Old Testament to prove to his readers that they did not even understand their own Law. He began with Leviticus 18:5 which states the purpose of the Law: if you obey it, you live.

"But we did obey it!" they would argue.

"You may have obeyed it *outwardly*," Paul would reply, "but you did not believe it from your heart." He then quoted Deuteronomy 30:12-14 and gave the passage a deeper spiritual meaning. The theme of Moses' message was "the commandment" (Deut. 30:11), referring to the Word of God. Moses argued that the Jews had no reason to disobey the Word of God because it had been clearly explained to them and it was not far from them. In fact, Moses urged them to receive the Word in their hearts. (See Deut. 5:29; 6:5-12; 13:3; and 30:6.) The emphasis in Deuteronomy is on the heart, the inner spiritual condition and not mere outward acts of obedience.

Paul gave us the spiritual understanding of this admonition. He saw "the commandment" or "the Word" as meaning "Christ, God's Word." So, he substituted "Christ" for "the commandment." He told us that God's way of salvation was not difficult and complicated. We do not have to go to heaven to find Christ, or into the world of the dead. He is

near to us. In other words, the Gospel of Christ—
the Word of faith—is available and accessible. The
sinner need not perform difficult works in order to
be saved. All he has to do is trust Christ. The very
Word on the lips of the religious Jews was the
Word of faith. The very Law that they read and
recited pointed to Christ.

At this point Paul quoted Isaiah 28:16 to show
that salvation is *by faith:* "Whosoever believeth on
Him shall not be ashamed." He quoted this verse
before in Romans 9:33. He made it clear in Romans
10:9-10 that salvation is *by faith*—we believe in the
heart, receive God's righteousness, and then confess Christ openly and without shame.

Paul's final quotation was from Joel 2:32, to
prove that this salvation is open to everyone: "For
whosoever shall call upon the name of the Lord
shall be saved." Paul had already proved that
"there is no difference" in condemnation (Rom.
3:20-23); now he affirms that "there is no difference" in salvation. Instead of the Jew having a
special righteousness of his own through the Law,
he was declared to be as much a sinner as the
Gentile that he condemned.

This entire section emphasizes the difference between "Law righteousness" and "faith righteousness." The contrasts are seen in the following sum-
mary.

Law Righteousness	*Faith Righteousness*
Only for the Jew	For "whosoever"
Based on works	Comes by faith alone
Self-righteousness	God's righteousness
Cannot save	Brings salvation
Tries to obey the Lord	Calls on the Lord
Leads to pride	Glorifies God

Having explained the reasons for Israel's rejection of God's righteousness, Paul moves into the next aspect of the subject.

2. The Remedy for Their Rejection (10:14-17)

This passage is often used as the basis for the Church's missionary program, and rightly so, but its first application is to the nation of Israel. The only way unbelieving Jews can be saved is by calling upon the Lord. But before they can call upon Him, they must believe. For the Jew, this meant believing that Jesus Christ of Nazareth truly is the Son of God and the Messiah of Israel. It also meant believing in His death and resurrection (Rom. 10:9-10). But in order to believe, they must hear the Word, for it is the Word that creates faith in the heart of the hearer (v. 17). This meant that a herald of the Word must be sent, and it is the Lord who does the sending. At this point, Paul could well have been remembering his own call to preach the Word to the Gentiles (Acts 13:1-3).

The quotation in Romans 10:15 is found in Isaiah 52:7 and Nahum 1:15. The Nahum reference had to do with the destruction of the Assyrian empire, the hated enemies of the Jews. Nineveh was their key city, a wicked city to which God had sent Jonah some 150 years before Nahum wrote. God had patiently dealt with Nineveh, but now His judgment was going to fall. It was this "good news" that the messenger brought to the Jews, and this is what made his feet so beautiful.

Isaiah used this statement for a *future* event— the return of Christ and the establishing of His glorious kingdom. "Thy God reigneth!" (Read Isa. 52:7-10.) The messenger with the beautiful feet announced that God had defeated Israel's enemies and that Messiah was reigning from Jerusalem.

But Paul used the quotation in a *present* application: the messengers of the Gospel taking the Good News to Israel today. The "peace" spoken of is "peace with God" (Rom. 5:1) and the peace Christ has effected between Jews and Gentiles by forming the one Body, the Church (Eph. 2:13-17). The remedy for Israel's rejection is in hearing the Word of the Gospel and believing on Jesus Christ.

Isaiah 53:1 was Paul's next quotation, proving that not all of Israel would obey His Word. This verse introduced one of the greatest Messianic chapters in the Old Testament. Traditionally, Jewish scholars have applied Isaiah 53 to the nation of Israel rather than to Messiah; but many ancient rabbis saw in it a picture of a suffering Messiah bearing the sins of His people. (See Acts 8:26-40.) In Isaiah's day, the people did not believe God's Word, nor do they believe it today. John 12:37-41 cites Isaiah 53:1 to explain how the nation saw Christ's miracles and still refused to believe. Because they would not believe, judgment came upon them and they could not believe.

Note that trusting Christ is not only a matter of believing, but also obeying. Not to believe on Christ is to disobey God. God "commandeth all men everywhere to repent" (Acts 17:30). Romans 6:17 also equates "believing" and "obeying." True faith must touch the will and result in a changed life.

We must never minimize the missionary outreach of the Church. While this passage relates primarily to Israel, it applies to all lost souls around the world. They cannot be saved unless they call upon the Lord Jesus Christ. But they cannot call unless they believe. Faith comes by hearing, so they must hear the message. How will they hear? A messenger must go to them with the message. But this means that God must call the messenger and the messenger must be sent. What a privilege it is to be one of His messengers and have beautiful feet!

As I was writing this chapter, my phone rang and one of the businessmen in our church reported another soul led to Christ. My caller had had serious spiritual problems a few years ago and I was able to help him. Since that time, he has led many to Christ, including some in his office. His phone call was to give me the good news that one of his associates had led a friend to Christ, another miracle in a spiritual chain reaction that has been going on for three years now. My friend has beautiful feet, and wherever he goes he shares the Good News of the Gospel.

Some of us share the news here at home, but others are sent to distant places. In spite of some closed doors, there are still more open doors for the Gospel than ever before; and we have better tools to work with. My friend Dr. E. Meyers Harrison, veteran missionary and professor of missions, says that there are four reasons why the Church must send out missionaries: (1) *the command from above*—"go ye into all the world . . ." (Mark 16:15); (2) *the cry from beneath*—"send him to my father's house" (Luke 16:27); (3) *the call from without*—"come over and help us" (Acts 16:9); and (4) *the constraint from within*—"the love of Christ constraineth us" (2 Cor. 5:14).

There remains a third aspect of Israel's rejection for Paul to discuss.

3. The Results of Their Rejection (10:18-21)
There are three results, and each of them is supported by a quotation from the Old Testament.

a. *Israel is guilty* (10:18)—Someone might have
argued with Paul: "But how do you know that Israel
really heard?" His reply would have been Psalm
19:4, a psalm that emphasizes the revelation of God
in the world. God reveals Himself in creation (Ps.
19:1-6) and in His Word (Ps. 19:7-11). The "Book
of Nature" and the "Book of Revelation" go together
and proclaim the glory of God. Israel had the benefit of both books, for she saw God at work in nature
and she received God's written Word. Israel heard,
but she would not *heed.* No wonder Jesus often had
to say to the crowds, "He that hath ears to hear, let
him hear!"

b. *The message goes to the Gentiles* (10:19-20)
—What marvelous grace! When Israel rejected her
Messiah, God sent the Gospel to the Gentiles that
they might be saved. This was predicted by Moses
in Deuteronomy 32:21. Paul had mentioned this
truth before in Romans 9:22-26. One reason why
God sent the Gospel to the Gentiles was that they
might provoke the Jews to jealousy (Rom. 10:19;
11:11). It was an act of grace both to the Jews and
to the Gentiles. The prophet Isaiah predicted, too,
that God would save the Gentiles (Isa. 65:1).

As you study the New Testament, you discover
that "to the Jew first" is a ruling principle of operation. Jesus began His ministry with the Jews. He
forbad His disciples to preach to the Gentiles or
the Samaritans when He sent them on their first
tour of ministry (Matt. 10:1-6). After His resurrection, He commanded them to wait in Jerusalem
and to start their ministry there (Luke 24:46-49;
Acts 1:8). In the first seven chapters of Acts, the
ministry is to Jews only, or to Gentiles who were
Jewish proselytes. But when the nation stoned
Stephen and persecution broke loose, God sent the

Gospel to the Samaritans (Acts 8:1-8), and then to the Gentiles (Acts 10).

The Jewish believers were shocked when Peter went to the Gentiles (Acts 11:1-18). But he explained that it was God who sent him and that it was clear to him that Jews and Gentiles were both saved the same way—by faith in Christ. But the opposition of the legalistic Jews was so great that the churches had to call a council to discuss the issue. The record of this council is given in Acts 15. Their conclusion was that Jews and Gentiles were all saved by faith in Christ, and that a Gentile did not have to become a Jewish proselyte before he could become a Christian.

c. *God still yearns over His people* (10:21)— This quotation is from Isaiah 65:2. "All day long" certainly refers to this present "day of salvation" or day of grace in which we live. While Israel as a nation has been set aside, individual Jewish people can be saved and are being saved. The phrase "all day long" makes us think of Paul's ministry to the Jews in Rome when he arrived there as a prisoner. "From morning till evening" Paul expounded the Scriptures to them and sought to convince them that Jesus is the Messiah (Acts 28:23). Through Paul, God was stretching out His arms of love to His disobedient people, yearning over them, and asking them to return. God's favor to the Gentiles did not change His love for the Jews.

God wants to use us to share the Gospel with both Jews and Gentiles. God can use our feet and our arms just as He used Paul's. Jesus Christ wept over Jerusalem and longed to gather His people in His arms! Instead, those arms were stretched out on a cross where He willingly died for Jews and Gentiles alike. God is long-suffering and patient "not willing that any should perish, but that all should come to repentance" (2 Peter 3:9).

Will God's patience with Israel wear out? Is there any future for the nation? Yes, there is, as the next chapter will show.

I say then, Hath God cast away His people? God forbid. For I also am an Israelite, of the seed of Abraham, of the tribe of Benjamin. [2] God hath not cast away His people which He foreknew. Wot ye not what the Scripture saith of Elias? How he maketh intercession to God against Israel, saying, [3] Lord they have killed Thy prophets, and digged down Thine altars; and I am left alone, and they seek my life. [4] But what saith the answer of God unto him? I have reserved to Myself seven thousand men, who have not bowed the knee to the image of Baal.   (Romans 11:1-4)

19 Thou wilt say then, The branches were broken off, that I might be grafted in. Well; because of unbelief they were broken off, and thou standest by faith. Be not highminded, but fear: [21] For if God spared not the natural branches, take heed lest He also spare not thee. [22] Behold therefore the goodness and severity of God: on them which fell, severity; but toward thee, goodness, if thou continue in His goodness: otherwise thou also shalt be cut off. [23] And they also, if they abide not still in unbelief, shall be grafted in: for God is able to graft them in again. [24] For if thou wert cut out of the olive tree which is wild by nature, and wert grafted contrary to nature into a good olive tree: how much more shall these, which be the natural branches, be grafted into their own olive tree? [25] For I would not, brethren, that ye should be ignorant of this mystery, lest ye should be wise in your own conceits; that blindness in part is happened to Israel, until the fulness of the Gentiles be come in.

(Romans 11:19-25)

10

God Is Not Through with Israel!

For centuries people have been puzzled by the nation of Israel. The Roman government recognized the Jewish religion, but it still called the nation *secta nefaria*—"a nefarious sect." The great historian Arnold Toynbee classified Israel as "a fossil civilization" and did not know what to do with it. For some reason, the nation did not fit into his historical theories.

Paul devoted all of Romans 11 to presenting proof that God is not through with Israel. We must not apply this chapter to the Church today, because Paul is discussing a literal future for a literal nation. He called five witnesses to prove there was a future in God's plan for the Jews.

1. Paul Himself (11:1)

"Hath God cast away His people? God forbid! For I also am an Israelite!" If God has cast away His people, then how can the conversion of the Apostle Paul be explained? The fact that his conversion is presented three times in the Book of Acts is significant (chaps. 9, 22, 26). Certainly Dr. Luke did not write these chapters and repeat the story just to exalt Paul. No, they were written to show Paul's conversion as an illustration of the future conversion of the nation of Israel. Paul called himself "one born out of due time" (1 Cor. 15:8). In 1 Timothy 1:16 he stated that God saved him "that in me first Jesus Christ might show forth all long-suffering, for a pattern to them which should hereafter believe on Him to life everlasting."

The accounts of Paul's conversion tell very little that parallels our salvation experience today. Certainly none of us has seen Christ in glory or actually heard Him speak from heaven. We were neither blinded by the light of heaven nor thrown to the ground. In what way, then, is Paul's conversion "a pattern"? It is a picture of how the nation of Israel will be saved when Jesus Christ returns to establish His kingdom on earth. The details of Israel's future restoration and salvation are given in Zechariah 12:10—13:1. The nation shall see Him as He returns (Zech. 14:4; Acts 1:11; Rev. 1:7), recognize Him as their Messiah, repent, and receive Him. It will be an experience similar to that of Saul of Tarsus when he was on his way to Damascus to persecute Christians (Acts 9).

This is why Paul used himself as the first witness. The fact that he was saved does not prove that there is a future for Israel. Rather, what is important is the *way* he was saved.

2. The Prophet Elijah (11:2-10)

Israel is God's elect nation; He foreknew them, or chose them, and they are His. The fact that most of the nation has rejected Christ is no proof that God has finished with His people. In his day, Elijah thought that the nation had totally departed from God. (Read 1 Kings 19.) But Elijah discovered that there was yet a remnant of true believers. He thought he was the only faithful Jew left and discovered that there were 7,000 more.

Paul referred to this "remnant" in Romans 9:27, a quotation from Isaiah 10:22-23. At no time has the entire nation of Israel been true to the Lord. God makes a distinction between Abraham's natural children and his spiritual children (Rom. 2:25-29). The fact that the Jews shared in the covenant by being circumcised did not guarantee their salvation. Like Abraham, they had to believe God in order to receive His righteousness (Rom. 4:1-5).

Note that this remnant is saved by grace and not by works (11:5-6). Note also the parallel in Rom. 9:30-33. It is impossible to mix grace and works, for the one cancels the other. Israel's main concern had always been in trying to please God with good works (Rom. 9:30—10:4). The nation refused to submit to Christ's righteousness, just as religious self-righteous people refuse to submit today.

If a remnant had been saved, thus proving that God was not through with His people, then what had happened to the rest of the nation? They had been hardened (a better translation than "blinded" in verse 7). This was the result of their resisting the truth, just as Pharaoh's heart was hardened because he resisted the truth. Paul quoted Isaiah

29:10 to support his statement, and also referred to Deuteronomy 29:4. We would expect a pagan ruler to harden himself against the Lord, but we do not expect God's people to do so.

Verses 9 and 10 are cited from Psalm 69:22-23. This psalm is one of the most important of the messianic Psalms and is referred to several times in the New Testament. Note especially verses 4, 9, 21, and 22. Their "table to become a snare" means that their blessings turn into burdens and judgments. This is what happened to Israel: their spiritual blessings should have led them to Christ, but instead they became a snare that kept them from Christ. Their very religious practices and observances became substitutes for the real experience of salvation. Sad to say, this same mistake is made today when people depend on religious rituals and practices instead of trusting in the Christ who is pictured in these activities.

Paul made it clear that the hardening of Israel is neither total nor final, and this is proof that God has a future for the nation. "Hardness in part is happened to Israel, until the fulness of the Gentiles be come in" (Rom. 11:25). The existence of the believing Jewish remnant today, as in Elijah's day, is evidence that God still has a plan for His people. Paul did not imitate Elijah's mistake and say "I only am left!" He knew that there was a remnant of Israel in this world who trusted God.

3. The Gentiles (11:11-15)

In Romans 2:1-3 Paul used the Gentiles to prove the Jews guilty of sin, but here he used the Gentiles to assure Israel of a future restoration. His logic here is beautiful. When the Jews rejected the Gospel, God sent it to the Gentiles and they believed

and were saved. Three tragedies occurred in
Israel: the nation *fell* (v. 11), was *lost* (v. 12,
"diminished"), and was *cast away* (v. 15). None
of these words suggests a *final* judgment on Israel.
But the amazing thing is that through Israel's fall,
salvation came to the Gentiles. God promised that
the Gentiles would be saved (Rom. 9:25-26) and
He kept His promise. Will He not also keep His
promise to the Jews?

It is important to understand that the Old Testament promises to the Gentiles were linked to
Israel's "rise"—her entering into her kingdom.
Prophecies like Isaiah 11 and Isaiah 60 make it
clear that the Gentiles will share in Israel's kingdom. But Israel did not "rise"; *she fell*! What would
God then do with the Gentiles? God introduced a
new factor—the Church—in which believing Jews
and Gentiles are one in Christ (Eph. 2:11-22). In
Ephesians 3, Paul called this new program "the
mystery," meaning "the sacred secret" that was not
revealed in the Old Testament. Does this mean
that God has abandoned His kingdom program for
Israel? Of course not! Israel is merely set aside until
the time comes for God's plans for Israel to be fulfilled.

Paul stated that the Gentiles had a vital ministry to Israel. Today, the saved Gentiles provoke
Israel "to jealousy" (see Rom. 10:19) because of
the spiritual riches they have in Christ. Israel today
is spiritually bankrupt, while Christians have "all
spiritual blessings" in Christ (Eph. 1:3). (If an
unsaved Jew visited the average church service,
would he be provoked *to jealousy* and wish he had
what we have—or would he just be provoked?)

There is a future for Israel. Paul calls it "their
fulness" (v. 12) and their "receiving" (v. 15).

Today, Israel is fallen spiritually, but when Christ returns, the nation will rise again. Today, Israel is cast away from God, but one day they shall be received again. God will never break His covenant with His people, and He has promised to restore them. (See Jer. 31:35-37 where God links His promises to Israel to the sun, moon, and stars.)

4. The Patriarchs (11:16-24)

From looking at the future, Paul next looked to the past to show Israel's spiritual heritage. From the beginning, Israel was a special people, set apart by God. Paul used two illustrations to prove his argument that God was not finished with the Jews.

a. *The lump of dough* (11:16a)—The reference here is to Numbers 15:17-21. The first part of the dough was to be offered up to God as a symbol that the entire lump belonged to Him. The same idea was involved in the Feast of Firstfruits, when the priest offered a sheaf to the Lord as a token that the entire harvest was His (Lev. 23:9-14). The basic idea is that when God accepts the part He sanctifies the whole.

Applying this to the history of Israel, we understand Paul's argument. God accepted the founder of the nation, Abraham, and in so doing set apart his descendants as well. God also accepted the other patriarchs, Isaac and Jacob, in spite of their sins or failings. This means that God must accept the "rest of the lump"—the nation of Israel.

b. *The olive tree* (11:16b-24)—This is a symbol of the nation of Israel (Jer. 11:16-17; Hosea 14:4-6). Please keep in mind that Paul was not discussing the relationship of individual believers to God, but the place of Israel in the plan of God. The roots of the tree support the tree; again, this was a symbol of the patriarchs who founded the nation. God made His covenants with Abraham, Isaac, and Jacob, and He cannot deny them or change them. Thus, it is God's promise to Abraham that sustains Israel even today.

Many of the Jewish people did not believe. Paul pictured them as branches broken off the tree. But he saw an amazing thing taking place: other branches were grafted into the tree to share in the life of the tree. These branches were the Gentiles. In verse 24, Paul described this "grafting in" as "contrary to nature." Usually a cultivated branch is grafted into a wild tree and shares its life without producing its poor fruit. But in this case, it was the "wild branch" (the Gentiles) that was grafted into the good tree! "Salvation is of the Jews" (John 4:22).

To say that the olive tree, with its natural and grafted branches, is a picture of the Church would be a great mistake. In the Church, "there is no difference"; believers are "all one in Christ Jesus" (Gal. 3:28). God does not look upon the members of Christ's Body and see them as Jews or Gentiles. The olive tree illustrates the relationship between Jew and Gentile in the program of God. The "breaking off of the branches" is the equivalent of "the fall" (v. 11), "the diminishing" (v. 12), and "the casting away" (v. 15). To read into this illustration the matter of the eternal destiny of the individual believer is to abuse the truth Paul was seeking to communicate.

Paul warned the Gentiles that they were obligated to Israel, and therefore they dared not boast of their new spiritual position (11:18-21). The Gentiles entered into God's plan because of faith, and not because of anything good they had done. Paul was discussing the Gentiles collectively, and not the individual experience of one believer or another.

It is worth noting that, according to Bible prophecy, the professing Gentile church will be "cut off" because of apostasy. First Timothy 4 and 2 Timothy 3, along with 2 Thessalonians 2, all indicate that the professing church in the last days will depart from the faith. *There is no hope for the apostate church, but there is hope for apostate Israel!* Why? Because of the roots of the olive tree. God will keep His promises to the patriarchs, but God will break off the Gentiles because of their unbelief.

No matter how far Israel may stray from the truth of God, the roots are still good. God is still the "God of Abraham, and the God of Isaac, and the God of Jacob" (Matt. 22:23; Ex. 3:6). He will keep His promises to these patriarchs. This means that the olive tree will flourish again!

5. God Himself (11:25-36)

Paul saved his best witness for the last. He proved that the very character and work of God were involved in the future of Israel. Men may dispute about prophecy and differ in their interpretations, but let every man realize that he is dealing with *God's people,* Israel.

a. *God's timing* (11:25)—What has happened to Israel is all a part of God's plan, and He knows what He is doing. The blinding (or hardening, v. 7) of Israel as a nation is neither total nor final: it is partial and temporary. How long will it last? "Until the fulness of the Gentiles be come in" (v. 25). There is a "fulness" for Israel (v. 12) and for the Gentiles. Today, God in His grace is visiting the Gentiles and taking out a people for His name (Acts 15:12-14). Individual Jews are being saved, of course; but this present age is primarily a time when God is visiting the Gentiles and building His Church. When this present age has run its course, and the fulness of the Gentiles has come in, then God will once more deal with the nation of Israel.

Romans 11:25 is one of several "*until* verses" in the Bible, all of which are important. Read Matthew 23:32-39, Luke 21:24, and Psalm 110:1 for other references. It is reassuring that God knows what time it is and that He is never late in fulfilling His will.

b. *God's promise* (11:26)—The reference here is Isaiah 59:20-21; and you ought to read Isaiah 60 to complete the picture. God has promised to save His people, and He will keep His promise. There are those who interpret this as meaning salvation to individuals through the Gospel, but it is my conviction that the prophet has national conversion in mind. "All Israel shall be saved" does not mean that every Jew who has ever lived will be converted, but that the Jews living when the Redeemer returns will see Him, receive Him, and be saved. Zechariah 12—13 give the details. It seems to me that there are too many details in these Old Testament prophecies of national restoration for Israel for us to spiritualize them and apply them to the Church today.

c. *God's covenant* (11:27-28). This is, of course, a continuation of the quotation from Isaiah 59; but the emphasis is on the covenant of God with Israel. God chose Israel in His grace and not because of any merit in her (Deut. 7:6-11 and 9:1-6). If the nation was not chosen because of its goodness, can it be rejected because of its sin?

"Election" means grace, not merit. The Jewish people are "enemies" to the believing Gentiles because
of their hostile attitude toward the Gospel. But to
God, the Jewish people are "beloved for the fathers'
sakes." God will not break His covenant with Abraham, Isaac, and Jacob.

d. *God's nature* (11:29)—"I am the Lord, I
change not" (Mal. 3:6). "God is not a man that He
should lie; neither the son of man, that He should
repent" (Num. 23:19). God's gifts to Israel, and
God's calling of Israel, cannot be taken back or
changed, or God would cease to be true to His own
perfect nature. The fact that Israel may not enjoy
her gifts, or live up to her privileges as an elect
nation, does not affect this fact one bit. God will
be consistent with Himself and true to His Word
no matter what men may do. "Shall their unbelief
make the faithfulness of God without effect?"
(Rom. 3:3, literal translation)

e. *God's grace* (11:30-32)—"Because of the unbelief of the Jews, you Gentiles were saved," said
Paul. "Now, may it be that through your salvation
Israel will come to know Christ." Note that Paul
repeatedly reminded the saved Gentiles that they
had a spiritual obligation to Israel to "provoke them
to jealousy" (Rom. 10:19, 11:11, 14). Israel's hardness is only "in part" (v. 25), which means that
individual Jews can be saved. God has included
"all in unbelief"—Jews and Gentiles—so that *all*
might have the opportunity to be saved by grace.
"There is no difference." If God can save Jews by
His grace and mercy today, why can He not save
them in the future?

We must remember that God chose the Jews so
that the Gentiles might be saved. "In thee shall
all families of the earth be blessed," was God's

promise to Abraham (Gen. 12:1-3). The tragedy was that Israel became exclusive and failed to share the truth with the Gentiles. They thought that the Gentiles had to become Jews in order to be saved. But God declared both Jews and Gentiles to be lost and condemned. This meant that He could have mercy on all because of the sacrifice of Christ on the cross.

f. *God's wisdom* (11:33-36)—Having contemplated God's great plan of salvation for Jews and Gentiles, all Paul could do was sing a hymn of praise. As someone has remarked, "Theology becomes doxology!" Only a God as wise as our God could take the fall of Israel and turn it into salvation for the world! His plans will not be aborted nor will His purposes lack fulfillment. No human being can fully know the mind of the Lord; and the more we study His ways, the more we offer Him praise. Are we to conclude that God does *not* know what He is doing, and that the nation of Israel completely ruined His plans? Of course not! God is too wise to make plans that will not be fulfilled. Israel did not allow Him to rule, so He overruled!

Paul summoned five witnesses, and they all agreed: there is a future for Israel. When Israel recovers from her "fall" and enters into her "fulness," the world will experience the riches of God's grace as never before. When Jesus Christ returns and sits on David's throne to reign over His kingdom, then Israel will be "reconciled" and "received," and it will be like a resurrection!

I beseech you therefore, brethren, by the mercies of God, that ye present your bodies a living sacrifice, holy, acceptable unto God, which is your reasonable service. [2] And be not conformed to this world: but be ye transformed by the renewing of your mind, that ye may prove what is that good, and acceptable, and perfect, will of God. [3] For I say, through the grace given unto me, to every man that is among you, not to think of himself more highly than he ought to think; but to think soberly, according as God hath dealt to every man the measure of faith.

(Romans 12:1-3)

9 Let love be without dissimulation. Abhor that which is evil; cleave to that which is good. [10] Be kindly affectioned one to another with brotherly love; in honor preferring one another; [11] Not slothful in business; fervent in spirit; serving the Lord; [12] Rejoicing in hope; patient in tribulation; continuing instant in prayer; [13] distributing to the necessity of saints; given to hospitality. [14] Bless them which persecute you: bless, and curse not.   (Romans 12:9-14)

Let every soul be subject unto the higher powers. For there is no power but of God: the powers that be are ordained of God. [2] Whosoever therefore resisteth the power, resisteth the ordinance of God: and they that resist shall receive to themselves damnation. [3] For rulers are not a terror to good works, but to the evil. Wilt thou then not be afraid of the power? do that which is good, and thou shalt have praise of the same: [4] For he is the minister of God to thee for good. But if thou do that which is evil, be afraid; for he beareth not the sword in vain: for he is the minister of God, a revenger to execute wrath upon him that doeth evil. [5] Wherefore ye must needs be subject, not only for wrath, but also for conscience sake.   (Romans 13:1-5)

11

Right Relationships Mean Right Living

In all of his letters, Paul concluded with a list of practical duties that were based on the doctrines he had discussed. In the Christian life, doctrine and duty always go together. What we believe helps to determine how we behave. It is not enough for us to understand Paul's doctrinal explanations. We must translate our *learning* into *living* and show by our daily lives that we trust God's Word.

The key idea in this section is *relationships*. The term "relational theology" is a relatively new one, but the idea is not new. If we have a right relationship to God, we will have a right relationship to the people who are a part of our lives. "If a man say, I love God, and hateth his brother, he is a liar" (1 John 4:20).

1. Our Relationship to God (12:1-2)

This is the fourth "therefore" in the letter. Romans 3:20 is the "therefore" of condemnation, declaring that the whole world is guilty before God. Romans 5:1 is the "therefore" of justification, and Romans 8:1 the "therefore" of assurance. In Romans 12:1, we have the "therefore" of dedication, and it is this dedication that is the basis for the other relationships that Paul discussed in this section.

What is true dedication? As Paul described it here, Christian dedication involves three steps.

a. *You give God your body* (12:1)—Before we trusted Christ, we used our body for sinful pleasures and purposes, but now that we belong to Him, we want to use our body for His glory. The Christian's body is God's temple (1 Cor. 6:19-20) because the Spirit of God dwells within him (Rom. 8:9). It is our privilege to glorify Christ in our body and magnify Christ in our body (Phil. 1:20-21).

Just as Jesus Christ had to take upon Himself a body in order to accomplish God's will on earth, so we must yield our bodies to Christ that He might continue God's work through us. We must yield the members of the body as "instruments of righteousness" (Rom. 6:13) for the Holy Spirit to use in the doing of God's work. The Old Testament sacrifices were dead sacrifices, but we are to be living sacrifices.

There are two "living sacrifices" in the Bible and they help us understand what this really means. The first is Isaac (Gen. 22); the second is our Lord Jesus

Christ. Isaac willingly put himself on the altar and would have died in obedience to God's will, but the Lord sent a ram to take his place. Isaac "died" just the same—He died to self and willingly yielded himself to the will of God. When he got off that altar, Isaac was a "living sacrifice" to the glory of God.

Of course, our Lord Jesus Christ is the perfect illustration of a "living sacrifice," because He actually died as a sacrifice, in obedience to His Father's will. But He arose again. And today He is in heaven as a "living sacrifice," bearing in His body the wounds of Calvary. He is our High Priest (Heb. 4:14-16) and our Advocate (1 John 2:1) before the throne of God.

The verb "present" in this verse means "present once and for all." It commands a definite commitment of the body to the Lord, just as a bride and groom in their wedding service commit themselves to each other. It is this once-for-all commitment that determines what they do with their bodies. Paul gives us two reasons for this commitment: (1) it is the right response to all that God has done for us— "I beseech you *therefore*, brethren, *by the mercies of God* . . ." (italics mine); and (2) this commitment is "our reasonable service" or "our spiritual worship. This means that every day is a worship experience when your body is yielded to the Lord.

b. *You give Him your mind* (12:2a)—The world wants to control your mind, but God wants to transform your mind. (See Eph. 4:17-24 and Col. 3:1-11.) This word *transform* is the same as *transfigure* in Matthew 17:2. It has come into our English language as the word "metamorphosis." It describes a change from within. The world wants to change your mind, so it exerts pressure from without. But the Holy Spirit changes your mind by releasing power from within. If the world controls your thinking, you are a *conformer;* if God controls your thinking, you are a *transformer.*

God transforms our minds and makes us spiritually minded by using His Word. As you spend time meditating on God's Word, memorizing it, and making it a part of your inner man, God will gradually make your mind more spiritual.

c. *You give Him your will* (12:2b)—Your mind controls your body, and your will controls your mind. Many people think they can control their will by "willpower," but usually they fail. (This was Paul's experience as recorded in Romans 7:15-21.) It is only when we yield the will to God that His power can take over and give us the willpower (and the won't power!) that we need to be victorious Christians.

We surrender our wills to God through disciplined prayer. As we spend time in prayer, we surrender our will to God and pray, with the Lord, "Not my will, but Thy will be done." We must pray about everything, and let God have His way in everything.

For many years I have tried to begin each day by surrendering my body to the Lord. Then I spend time with His Word and let Him transform my mind and prepare my thinking for that new day. Then I pray, and I yield the plans of the day to Him and let Him work as He sees best. I especially pray about those tasks that upset or worry me—and He always sees me through. To have a right relationship with God, we must start the day by yielding to Him our bodies, minds, and wills.

2. Relationship to Other Believers (12:3-16)
Paul was writing to Christians who were members

of local churches in Rome. He described their relationship to each other in terms of the members of a body. (He used this same picture in 1 Corinthians 12 and Ephesians 4:7-16.) The basic idea is that each believer is a living part of Christ's Body, and each one has a spiritual function to perform. Each believer has a gift (or gifts) to be used for the building up of the Body and the perfecting of the other members of the Body. In short, we belong to each other, we minister to each other, and we need each other. What are the essentials for spiritual ministry and growth in the Body of Christ?

a. *Honest evaluation* (12:3)—Each Christian must know what his spiritual gifts are and what ministry (or ministries) he is to have in the local church. It is not wrong for a Christian to recognize gifts in his own life and in the lives of others. What *is* wrong is the tendency to have a false evaluation of ourselves, Nothing causes more damage in a local church than a believer who overrates himself and tries to perform a ministry that he cannot do. (Sometimes the opposite is true, and people undervalue themselves. Both attitudes are wrong.)

The gifts that we have came because of God's grace. They must be accepted and exercised by faith. We were saved "by grace, through faith" (Eph. 2:8-9), and we must live and serve "by grace through faith." Since our gifts are from God, we cannot take the credit for them. All we can do is accept them and use them to honor His Name. (See 1 Corinthians 15:10 for Paul's personal testimony about gifts.)

I once ministered with two men who had opposite attitudes toward their gifts: the one man constantly belittled his gifts and would not use them, and the other man constantly boasted about gifts that he did not possess. Actually, both of them were guilty of pride, because both of them refused to acknowledge God's grace and let Him have the glory. Moses made a similar mistake when God called him (Ex. 4:1-13). When the individual believers in a church know their gifts, accept them by faith, and use them for God's glory, then God can bless in a wonderful way.

b. *Faithful cooperation* (12:4-8)—Each believer has a different gift, and God has bestowed these gifts so the local Body can grow in a balanced way. But each Christian must exercise his or her gift by faith. We may not see the result of our ministry, but the Lord sees it and He blesses. Note that "exhortation" (encouragement) is just as much a spiritual ministry as preaching or teaching. Giving and showing mercy are also important gifts. To some people, God has given the ability to rule, or to administer the various functions of the church. Whatever gift we have must be dedicated to God and used for the good of the whole church.

It is tragic when any one gift is emphasized in a local church beyond all the other gifts. "Are all apostles? are all prophets? are all teachers? are all workers of miracles? have all the gifts of healing? do all speak with tongues? do all interpret?" (1 Cor. 12:29-30) The answer to all these questions is no! And for a Christian to minimize the other gifts while he emphasizes his own gift is to deny the very purpose for which gifts are given: the benefit of the whole Body of Christ. "Now to each man the manifestation of the Spirit is given for the common good" (1 Cor. 12:7, NIV).

Spiritual gifts are tools to build with, not toys to play with or weapons to fight with. In the church at Corinth, the believers were tearing down the ministry because they were abusing spiritual gifts. They were using their gifts as ends in themselves and not as a means toward the end of building up the church. They so emphasized their spiritual gifts that they lost their spiritual graces! They had the gifts of the Spirit but were lacking in the fruit of the spirit—love, joy, peace, etc. (Gal. 5:22-23)

c. *Loving participation* (12:9-16)—Here the emphasis is on the attitudes of those who exercise the spiritual gifts. It is possible to use a spiritual gift in an unspiritual way. Paul makes this same point in 1 Corinthians 13, the great "love chapter" of the New Testament. Love is the circulatory system of the spiritual Body, which enables all the members to function in a healthy, harmonious way. This must be an honest love, not a hypocritical love (v. 9); and it must be humble, not proud (v. 10). "Preferring one another" means treating others as more important than ourselves (Phil. 2:1-4).

Serving Christ usually means Satanic opposition and days of discouragement. Paul admonished his readers to maintain their spiritual zeal because they were serving the Lord and not men. When life becomes difficult, the Christian cannot permit his zeal to grow cold. "Be joyful in hope, patient in affliction, faithful in prayer" (Rom. 12:12, NIV).

Finally, Paul reminds them that they must enter into the feelings of others. Christian fellowship is much more than a pat on the back and a handshake. It means sharing the burdens and the blessings of others so that we all grow together and glorify the Lord. If Christians cannot get along with one another, how can they ever face their enemies? A humble attitude and a willingness to share are the marks of a Christian who truly ministers to the Body. Our Lord ministered to the common people, and they heard Him gladly (Mark 12:37). When a local church decides it wants only a certain "high class" of people, it departs from the Christian ideal for ministry.

3. Our Relationship to Our Enemies (12:17-21)

The believer who seeks to obey God is going to have his enemies. When our Lord was ministering on earth, He had enemies. No matter where Paul and the other apostles traveled, there were enemies who opposed their work. Jesus warned His disciples that their worst enemies might be those of their own household (Matt. 10:36). Unfortunately, some believers have enemies because they lack love and patience, and not because they are faithful in their witness. There is a difference between sharing in "the offense of the cross" (Gal. 5:11; 6:12-15) and being an offensive Christian!

The Christian must not play God and try to avenge himself. Returning evil for evil, or good for good, is the way most people live. But the Christian must live on a higher level. And return good for evil. Of course, this requires *love,* because our first inclination is to fight back. It also requires *faith,* believing that God can work and accomplish His will in our lives and in the lives of those who hurt us. We must give place to "the wrath"—the wrath of God (Deut. 32:35).

A friend of mine once heard a preacher criticize him over the radio and tell things that were not only unkind, but also untrue. My friend became very angry and was planning to fight back, when a godly preacher said, "Don't do it. If you defend yourself, then the Lord can't defend you. Leave it in His hands." My friend followed that wise counsel, and the Lord vindicated him.

The admonition in Romans 12:20 reminds us of Christ's words in Matthew 5:44-48. These words are easy to read but difficult to practice. Surely we need to pray and ask God for love as we try to show kindness to our enemies. Will they take advantage of us? Will they hate us more? Only the Lord knows. Our task is not to protect ourselves but to obey the Lord and leave the results with Him. Paul referred to Proverbs 25:21-22 as he urged us to return good for evil in the name of the Lord. The "coals of fire" refer perhaps to the feeling of shame our enemies will experience when we return good for evil.

As children of God, we must live on the highest level—returning good for evil. Anyone can return good for good and evil for evil. The only way to overcome evil is with good. If we return evil for evil, we only add fuel to the fire. And even if our enemy is not converted, we have still experienced the love of God in our own hearts and have grown in grace.

4. Our Relationship to the State (Romans 13:1-14)

God has established three institutions: the home (Gen. 2:18-25), government (Gen. 9:1-17), and the church (Acts 2). Paul was writing to believers at the very heart of the Roman Empire. As yet, the great persecutions had not started, but were on the way. Christianity was still considered a Jewish sect, and the Jewish religion was approved by Rome. But the day would come when it would be very difficult, if not impossible, for a Christian to be loyal to the Emperor. He could not drop incense on the altar and affirm, "Caesar is god!"

In our own day, we have people who teach riot and rebellion *in the name of Christ!* They would have us believe that the Christian thing to do is to disobey the law, rebel against the authorities, and permit every man to do that which is right in his own eyes. Paul refuted this position in this chapter by explaining four reasons why the Christian must be in subjection to the laws of the State.

a. *For wrath's sake* (13:1-4)—It is God who has established the governments of the world (see Acts 17:24-28). This does not mean that He is responsible for the sins of tyrants, but only that the authority to rule comes originally from God. It was this lesson that Nebuchadnezzar had to learn the hard way. (See Daniel 4, and especially verses 17, 25, and 32.) To resist the law is to resist the God who established government in the world, and this means inviting punishment.

Rulers must bear the sword; that is, they have the power to afflict punishment and even to take life. God established human government because man is a sinner and must have some kind of authority over him. God has given the sword to rulers, and with it the authority to punish and even to execute. Capital punishment was ordained in Genesis 9:5-6, and it has not been abolished. Even though we cannot always respect the man in office, we must respect the office, for government was ordained by God.

On more than one occasion in his ministry, Paul used the Roman law to protect his life and to extend his work. The centurions mentioned in the Book of Acts appear to be men of character and high ideals. Even though government officials are not believers, they are still the "ministers of God" because He established the authority of the State.

b. *For conscience' sake* (13:5-7)—We move a bit higher in our motivation now. Any citizen can obey the law because of fear of punishment, but a Christian ought to obey because of conscience. Of course, if the government interferes with conscience, then the Christian must obey God rather than men (Acts 5:29). But when the law is right, the Christian must obey it if he is to maintain a good conscience (1 Tim. 1:5, 19; 3:9; 4:2; and Acts 24:16).

The United States Government maintains a "Conscience Fund" for people who want to pay their debts to the Government and yet remain anonymous. Some city governments have a similar fund. I read about a city that had investigated some tax frauds and announced that several citizens were going to be indicted. They did not release the names of the culprits. That week, a number of people visited the City Hall to "straighten out their taxes"—and many of them were not on the indictment list. When conscience begins to work, we cannot live with ourselves until we have made things right.

Verse 7 commands us to pay what we owe: taxes, revenue, respect, honor. If we do not pay our taxes, we show disrespect to the law, the officials, and the Lord. And this cannot but affect the conscience of the believer. We may not agree with all that is done with the money we pay in taxes, but we dare not violate our conscience by refusing to pay.

c. *For love's sake* (13:8-10)—Paul enlarged the circle of responsibility by including other people besides government officials. "Love one another" is the basic principle of the Christian life. It is the "new commandment" that Christ gave to us (John 13:34). When we practice love, there is no need for any other laws, because love covers it all! If we love others, we will not sin against them. This explained why the Ten Commandments were not referred to often in the New Testament. In fact, the Sabbath commandment is not quoted at all in any of the epistles. As believers, we do not live under the Law; we live under grace. Our motive for obeying God and helping others is the love of Christ in our hearts.

Does "Owe no man anything" refer also to the Christian's financial practices? Some people believe that it does, and that it is a sin to have a debt. J. Hudson Taylor, the godly missionary to China, would never incur a debt, basing his conviction on this verse. Charles Spurgeon, the great Baptist preacher, had the same conviction. However, the Bible does not forbid borrowing or legal financial transactions that involve interest. What the Bible does forbid is the charging of high interest, robbing the brethren, and failing to pay honest debts. (See Ex. 22:25-27 and Neh. 5:1-11.) Matthew 25:27 and Luke 19:23 indicate that banking and investing for gain are not wrong. Certainly no one should get into unnecessary debt, or sign contracts he cannot maintain. "Thou shalt not steal." But to make Romans 13:8 apply to all kinds of legal obligations involving money is, to me, stretching a point.

In this section, Paul has centered on the very heart of the problem—the human heart. Because the heart of man is sinful, God established government. But laws cannot change the heart; man's heart is still selfish and can be changed only by the grace of God.

d. *For Jesus' sake* (13:11-14)—We have come a long way in our reasons for obeying the law: from fear to conscience to love to our devotion to Jesus Christ! The emphasis is on the imminent return of Christ. As His servants, we want to be found faithful when He returns. The completion of our salvation is near! The light is dawning! Therefore, be ready!

Paul gave several admonitions in the light of the Lord's soon return. The first is, "Wake up!" Relate this with 1 Thessalonians 5:1-11, and also Matthew 25:1-13. The second is, "Clean up!" We do not want to be found dressed in dirty garments when the Lord returns (1 John 2:28—3:3). The Christian wears the armor of light, not the deeds of darkness. He has no reason to get involved in the sinful pleasures of the world. Finally, Paul admonished, "Grow up!" (v. 14) To "put on" the Lord Jesus Christ means to become more like Him, to receive by faith all that He is for our daily living. We grow on the basis of the food that we eat. This is why God warns us not to make provisions for the flesh. If we feed the flesh, we will fail; but if we feed the inner man the nourishing things of the Spirit, we will succeed.

In other words, a Christian citizen ought to be the best citizen. Christians may not always agree on politics or parties, but they can all agree on their attitude toward human government.

Him that is weak in the faith receive ye, but not to doubtful disputations. [2] For one believeth that he may eat all things: another, who is weak, eateth herbs. [3] Let not him that eateth despise him that eateth not; and let not him which eateth not judge him that eateth: for God hath received him.

(Romans 14:1-3)

7 For none of us liveth to himself, and no man dieth to himself. [8] For whether we live, we live unto the Lord; and whether we die, we die unto the Lord: whether we live therefore, or die, we are the Lord's. [9] For to this end Christ both died, and rose, and revived, that He might be Lord both of the dead and the living. [10] But why dost thou judge thy brother or why dost thou set at nought thy brother? for we shall all stand before the judgment seat of Christ.

(Romans 14:7-10)

14 I know, and am persuaded by the Lord Jesus, that there is nothing unclean of itself: but to him that esteemeth any thing to be unclean, to him it is unclean. [15] But if thy brother be grieved with thy meat, now walkest thou not charitably. Destroy not him with thy meat, for whom Christ died. [16] Let not then your good be evil spoken of: [17] For the kingdom of God is not meat and drink; but righteousness, and peace, and joy in the Holy Ghost. (Romans 14:14-17)

1. We then that are strong ought to bear the infirmities of the weak, and not to please ourselves. [2] Let every one of us please his neighbour for his good to edification [3] For even Christ pleased not Himself; but, as it is written, the reproaches of them that reproached thee fell on me.

(Romans 15:1-3)

12

When Christians Disagree

Disunity has always been a major problem with God's people. Even the Old Testament records the civil wars and family fights among the people of Israel, and almost every local church mentioned in the New Testament had divisions to contend with. The Corinthians were divided over human leaders, and some of the members were even suing each other (1 Cor. 1:10-13; 6:1-8). The Galatian saints were "biting and devouring" one another (Gal. 5:15), and the saints in Ephesus and Colosse had to be reminded of the importance of Christian unity (Eph. 4:1-3; Col. 2:1-2). In the church at Philippi, two women were at odds with each other and, as a result, were splitting the church (Phil. 4:1-3). No wonder the psalmist wrote, "Behold, how good and how pleasant it is for brethren to dwell together in unity" (Ps. 133:1).

Some of these problems stemmed from the backgrounds of the believers in the churches. The Jews, for example, were saved out of a strict legalistic background that would be difficult to forget. The Gentiles never had to worry about diets and days. The first church council in history debated the issue of the relationship of the Christian to the Law (Acts 15).

The believers in Rome were divided over special diets and special days. Some of the members thought it was a sin to eat meat, so they ate only vegetables. Other members thought it a sin not to observe the Jewish holy days. If each Christian had kept his convictions to himself, there would have been no problem, but they began to criticize and judge one another. The one group was sure the other group was not at all spiritual.

Unfortunately, we have similar problems today with many "grey areas" of life that are not clearly right or wrong to every believer. Some activities we know are wrong, because the Bible clearly condemns them. Other activities we know are right, because the Bible clearly commands them. But when it comes to areas that are not clearly defined in Scripture, we find ourselves needing some other kind of guidance. Paul gave principles of this guidance. He explained how believers could disagree on non-essentials and still maintain unity in the church. He gave his readers three important admonitions.

1. Receive One Another (14:1-12)
You will note that this section begins and ends with this admonition (Rom. 15:7). Paul was addressing those who were "strong in the faith," that is, those who understood their spiritual liberty in Christ and were not enslaved to diets or holy days. The "weak in faith" were immature believers who

felt obligated to obey legalistic rules concerning what they ate and when they worshiped. Many people have the idea that the Christians who follow strict rules are the most mature, but this is not necessarily the case. In the Roman assemblies, the weak Christians were those who clung to the Law and did not enjoy their freedom in the Lord. The weak Christians were judging and condemning the strong Christians, and the strong Christians were despising the weak Christians.

"Welcome one another!" was Paul's first admonition; and he gave four reasons why they should:

a. *God has received us* (14:1-3)—It is not our responsibility to decide the requirements for Christian fellowship in a church; only the Lord can do this. To set up man-made restrictions on the basis of personal prejudices (or even convictions) is to go beyond the Word of God. Because God has received us, we must receive one another. We must not argue over these matters, nor must we judge or despise one another. Perhaps St. Augustine put the matter best: "In essentials, unity; in nonessentials, liberty; in all things, charity."

When God sent Peter to take the Gospel to the Gentiles, the church criticized Peter because he ate with these new Christians (Acts 11:1-3). But God had clearly revealed His acceptance of the Gentiles by giving them the same Holy Spirit that He bestowed upon the Jewish believers at Pentecost (Acts 10:44-48; 11:15-18). Peter did not obey this truth consistently, for later on he refused to fellowship with the Gentile Christians in Antioch, and Paul had to rebuke him (Gal. 2:11-13). God showed both Peter and Paul that Christian fellowship was not to be based on food or religious calendars.

In every church there are weak and strong believers. The strong understand spiritual truth and practice it, but the weak have not yet grown into that level of maturity and liberty. The weak must not condemn the strong and call them unspiritual. The strong must not despise the weak and call them immature. God has received both the weak and the strong; therefore, they should receive one another.

b. *God sustains His own* (12:4)—The strong Christian was judged by the weak Christian, and this Paul condemned because it was wrong for the weak Christian to take the place of God in the life of the strong Christian. God is the Master; the Christian is the servant. It is wrong for anyone to interfere with this relationship.

It is encouraging to know that our success in the Christian life does not depend on the opinions or attitudes of other Christians. God is the Judge, and He is able to make us stand. The word "servant" here suggests that Christians ought to be busy working for the Lord; then they will not have the time or inclination to judge or condemn other Christians. People who are busy winning souls to Christ have more important things to do than to investigate the lives of the saints!

c. *Jesus Christ is Lord* (14:5-9)—The word "Lord" is found eight times in these verses. No Christian has the right to "play God" in another Christian's life. We can pray, advise, and even admonish, but we cannot take the place of God. What is it that makes a dish of food "holy" or a day "holy"? It is the fact that we relate it to the Lord. The person who treats a special day as "holy" does so "unto the Lord." The person who treats every day as sacred, does so "unto the

Lord." The Christian who eats meat gives thanks to the Lord, and the Christian who abstains from meat abstains "unto the Lord." To be "fully persuaded—or assured—in his own mind" (v. 5) means: Let every man see to it that he is really doing what he does for the Lord's sake, and not merely on the basis of some prejudice or whim.

Some standards and practices in our local churches are traditional but not necessarily scriptural. Some of us can remember when dedicated Christians opposed Christian radio "because Satan was the prince of the power of the air!" Fashions change from year to year. Christians no longer need to fight about Hollywood movies because television brings them right into the home. Some people even make Bible translations a test of orthodoxy. The church is divided and weakened because Christians will not allow Jesus Christ to be Lord.

An interesting illustration of this truth is given in John 21:15-25. Jesus had restored Peter to his place as an apostle, and once again He told him, "Follow Me." Peter began to follow Christ, but then he heard someone walking behind him. It was the Apostle John.

Then Peter asked Jesus, "Lord, what shall this man do?"

Notice the Lord's reply: "What is that to thee? Follow thou Me!" In other words, "Peter, you make sure you have made Me Lord of your Life. Let Me worry about John." Whenever I hear believers condemning other Christians because of something they disagree with, something that is not essential or forbidden in the Word, I feel like saying, "What is that to thee? Follow Christ! Let Him be the Lord!"

Paul emphasized the believer's union with Christ: "Whether we live, therefore, or whether we die, we are the Lord's" (v. 8). Our first responsibility is to the Lord. If Christians would go to the Lord in prayer instead of going to their brother with criticism, there would be stronger fellowship in our churches.

d. *Jesus Christ is Judge* (14:10-12)—Paul asked the weak Christian, "Why are you judging your brother?" Then he asked the strong Christian, "Why are you despising your brother?" Both strong and weak must stand at the judgment seat of Christ, and they will not judge each other—they will be judged by the Lord.

The judgment seat of Christ is that place where Christians will have their works judged by the Lord. It has nothing to do with our sins, since Christ has paid for them and they can be held against us no more (Rom. 8:1). The word for "judgment seat" in the Greek is *bema,* meaning the place where the judges stood at the athletic games. If during the games they saw an athlete break the rules, they immediately disqualified him. At the end of the contests, the judges gave out the rewards. (See 1 Cor. 9:24-27.) First Corinthians 3:10-15 gives another picture of the judgment seat of Christ. Paul compared our ministries with the building of a temple. If we build with cheap materials, the fire will burn them up. If we use precious, lasting materials, our works will last. If our works pass the test, we receive a reward. If they are burned up, we lose the reward, but we are still saved "yet so as by fire."

How does the Christian prepare for the judgment seat of Christ? By making Jesus Christ Lord of his life and faithfully obeying Him. Instead of judging other Christians, we had better judge our own lives and make sure we are ready to meet Christ at the bema. (See Luke 12:41-48, Hebrews 13:17, and 1 John 2:28.)

The fact that our sins will never be brought up against us should not encourage us to disobey God. Sin in our lives keeps us from serving Christ as we should, and this means loss of reward. Lot is a good example of this truth (Gen. 18—19). Lot was not walking with the Lord as was his uncle, Abraham and, as a result, he lost his testimony even with his own family. When the judgment finally came, Lot was spared the fire and brimstone, but everything he lived for was burned up. He was saved "yet so as by fire."

Paul explained that they did not have to give an account for anyone else but themselves. So they were to make sure that their account would be a good one. He was stressing the principle of Lordship—make Jesus Christ the Lord of your life, and let Him be the Lord in the lives of other Christians as well.

Two of the most famous Christians in the Victorian Era in England were Charles Spurgeon and Joseph Parker, both of them mighty preachers of the Gospel. Early in their ministries they fellowshiped and even exchanged pulpits. Then they had a disagreement, and the reports even got into the newspapers. Spurgeon accused Parker of being unspiritual because he attended the theater. Interestingly enough, Spurgeon smoked cigars, a practice many believers would condemn. Who was right? Who was wrong? Perhaps *both* of them were wrong! When it comes to questionable matters in the Christian life, cannot dedicated believers disagree without being disagreeable? "I have learned that

God blesses people I disagree with!" a friend of mine told me one day, and I have learned the same thing. When Jesus Christ is Lord, we permit Him to deal with His own servants as He wishes.

2. Edify One Another (14:13-23)

If we stopped with the first admonition, it might give the impression that Christians were to leave each other alone and let the weak remain weak. But this second admonition explains things further. The emphasis is not on "master-servant" but on "brother." It is the principle of brotherly love. If we love each other, we will seek to edify each other, build each other up in the faith. Paul shared several facts to help his readers help their brethren.

a. *Christians affect each other* (14:13-15)—Note the possible ways we can affect each other. We can cause others to stumble, grieve others, or even destroy others. Paul was speaking of the way the strong Christian affected the weak Christian. Paul dealt with a similar problem in 1 Corinthians 8—9, where the question was, "Should Christians eat meat that has been offered to idols in heathen temples?" There he pointed out that knowledge and love must work together. "Knowledge puffs up, but love builds up" (1 Cor. 8:1, NIV). The strong Christian has spiritual knowledge, but if he does not practice love, his knowledge will hurt the weak Christian. Knowledge must be balanced by love.

Often little children are afraid of the dark and think there is something hiding in the closet. Of course, mother knows that the child is safe; but her knowledge alone cannot assure or comfort the child. You can never argue a child into losing fear. When the mother sits at the bedside, talks lovingly to the child, and assures him that everything is secure, then the child can go to sleep without fear. Knowledge plus love helps the weak person grow strong.

"There is nothing unclean of itself," Paul wrote (v. 14). No foods are unclean, no days are unclean, no people are unclean. (Read Acts 10 to see how Peter learned this lesson.) What something *does* to a person determines its quality. One man may be able to read certain books and not be bothered by them, while a weaker Christian reading the same books might be tempted to sin. But the issue is not "How does it affect me?" so much as "If I do this, how will it affect my brother?" Will it make him stumble? Will it grieve him or even destroy him by encouraging him to sin? Is it really worth it to harm a brother just so I can enjoy some food? No!

b. *Christians must have priorities* (14:16-18)— Like the Pharisees of old, we Christians have a way of majoring in the minor (Matt. 23:23-24). I have seen churches divided over matters that were really insignificant when compared with the vital things of the Christian faith. I have heard of churches being split over such minor matters as the location of the piano in the auditorium and the serving of meals on Sundays. "The kingdom of God is not meat and drink . . ." (v. 17). "But food does not bring us near to God; we are no worse if we do not eat, and no better if we do" (1 Cor. 8:8, NIV).

Not the externals, but the eternals must be first in our lives: righteousness, peace, and joy. Where do they come from? The Holy Spirit of God at work in our lives. (See Rom. 5:1-2.) If each believer would yield to the Spirit and major in a godly life, we would not have Christians fighting with each other over minor matters. Spiritual priorities are essential to harmony in the church.

c. *Christians must help each other grow* (14: 19-21). Both the strong believer and the weak believer need to grow. The strong believer needs to grow in *love*; the weak believer needs to grow in *knowledge*. So long as a brother is weak in the faith, we must lovingly deal with him in his immaturity. But if we really love him, we will help him to grow. It is wrong for a Christian to remain immature, having a weak conscience.

An illustration from the home might help us better understand what is involved. When a child comes into a home, everything has to change. Mother and father are careful not to leave the scissors on the chair or anything dangerous within reach. But as the child matures, it is possible for the parents to adjust the rules of the house and deal with him in a more adult fashion. It is natural for a child to stumble when he is learning to walk. But if an adult constantly stumbles, we know something is wrong.

Young Christians need the kind of fellowship that will protect them and encourage them to grow. But we cannot treat them like "babies" all their lives! The older Christians must exercise love and patience and be careful not to cause them to stumble. But the younger Christians must "grow in grace and in the knowledge of our Lord and Saviour Jesus Christ" (2 Peter 3:18). As they mature in the faith, they can help other believers to grow. To gear the ministry of a Sunday School class or local church only to the baby Christians is to hinder their growth as well as the ministry of the more mature saints. The weak must learn from the strong, and the strong must love the weak. The result will be peace and maturity to the glory of God.

d. *Christians must not force their opinions on others* (14:22-23)—There are certain truths that all Christians must accept because they are the foundation for the faith. But areas of honest disagreement must not be made a test of fellowship. If you have a sincere conviction from God about a matter, keep it to yourself and do not try to force everybody else to accept it. No Christian can "borrow" another Christian's convictions and be honest in his Christian life. Unless he can hold them and practice them "by faith," he is sinning. Even if a person's convictions are immature, he must never violate his conscience. This would do great damage to his spiritual life. For example, the mature Christian knows that an idol is nothing. But a young Christian, just converted out of pagan idolatry, would still have fears about idols. If the strong believer forced the new Christian to eat meat sacrificed to an idol, the younger Christian would experience problems in his conscience that would only further weaken it. (See 1 Cor. 8—9.)

Conscience is strengthened by knowledge. But knowledge must be balanced by love; otherwise it tears down instead of building up. The truth that "all foods are clean" (vv. 14, 20) will not of itself make a Christian grow. When this truth is taught in an atmosphere of love, then the younger Christian can grow and develop a strong conscience. Believers may hold different convictions about many matters, but they must hold them in love.

3. Please One Another (15:1-7)

Paul classified himself with the strong saints as he dealt with a basic problem—*selfishness*. True

Christian love is not selfish; rather, it seeks to share with others and make others happy. It is even willing to carry the younger Christians, to help them along in their spiritual development. We do not endure them. We encourage them!

Of course, the great example in this is our Lord Jesus Christ. He paid a tremendous price in order to minister to us. Paul quoted Psalm 69:9 to prove his point. Does a strong Christian think he is making a great sacrifice by giving up some food or drink? Then let him measure his sacrifice by the sacrifice of Christ. No sacrifice we could ever make could match Calvary.

A person's spiritual maturity is revealed by his discernment. He is willing to give up his rights that others might be helped. He does this, not as a burden, but as a blessing. Just as loving parents make sacrifices for their children, so the mature believer sacrifices to help younger Christians grow in the faith.

Paul shared the two sources of spiritual power from which we must draw if we are to live to please others: the Word of God (v. 4) and prayer (vv. 5-6). We must confess that we sometimes get impatient with younger Christians, just as parents become impatient with their children. But the Word of God can give us the "patience and encouragement" that we need. Paul closed this section praying for his readers, that they might experience from God that spiritual unity that He alone can give.

This suggests to us that the local church must major in the Word of God and prayer. The first real danger to the unity of the church came because the apostles were too busy to minister God's Word and pray (Acts 6:1-7). When they found others to share their burdens, they returned to their proper ministry, and the church experienced harmony and growth.

The result of this is, of course, glory to God (v. 7). Disunity and disagreement do not glorify God; they rob Him of glory. Abraham's words to Lot are applicable to today: "Let there be no strife, I pray thee, between me and thee . . . for we be brethren" (Gen. 13:8). The neighbors were watching! Abraham wanted them to see that he and Lot were different because they worshiped the true God. In His prayer in John 17, Jesus prayed for the unity of the church to the glory of God (John 17:20-26).

Receive one another; edify one another; and please one another—all to the glory of God.

8 Now I say that Jesus Christ was a minister of the circumcision for the truth of God, to confirm the promises made unto the fathers: [9] And that the Gentiles might glorify God for His mercy: as it is written, For this cause I will confess to Thee among the Gentiles, and sing unto Thy name. [10] And again he saith, Rejoice, ye Gentiles, with His people. [11] And again, Praise the Lord, all ye Gentiles; and laud Him, all ye people. [12] And again, Esaias saith, There shall be a root of Jesse, and He that shall rise to reign over the Gentiles; in Him shall the Gentiles trust. [13] Now the God of hope fill you with all joy and peace in believing, that ye may abound in hope, through the power of the Holy Ghost. [14] And I myself also am persuaded of you, my brethren, that ye also are full of goodness, filled with all knowledge, and able also to admonish one another. [15] Nevertheless, brethren, I have written the more boldly unto you in some sort, as putting you in mind, because of the grace that is given to me of God. [16] That I should be the minister of Jesus Christ to the Gentiles, ministering the Gospel of God, that the offering up of the Gentiles might be acceptable, being sanctified by the Holy Ghost.   (Romans 15:8-16)

25 Now to Him that is of power to stablish you according to my Gospel, and the preaching of Jesus Christ, according to the revelation of the mystery, which was kept secret since the world began, [26] But now is made manifest, and by the Scriptures of the prophets, according to the commandment of the everlasting God, made known to all nations for the obedience of faith: [27] To God only wise, be glory through Jesus Christ for ever. Amen.   (Romans 16:25-27)

13

Man on
the Move

One of the key words in the closing chapters of Romans is "ministry." In fact, Paul used three different Greek words to discuss the theme. In Romans 15:8, 25, 31, and 16:1, it is the simple word for a servant or service. Our English word "deacon" comes from this word. In verses 16 and 27 (the word "minister"), he used the ordinary word for service in public office or in the temple. In Romans 15:16 he used a word that is found nowhere else in the Greek New Testament; and it means "to perform sacred rites, to minister in a priestly service."

In this section, Paul explained four different ministries.

1. The Ministry of Jesus Christ to the Gentiles (15:8-13)

The supreme example of ministry must always be Jesus Christ. "But I am among you as he that serveth" (Luke 22:27). He came first of all to minister to the Jews, that through Israel He might be able to minister to the Gentiles. "To the Jew first" is a principle that was followed in the earthly ministry of Christ and in the early ministry of the Church.

For example, John the Baptist came to minister to the nation of Israel to prepare them for their Messiah. When Jesus began His ministry, it was only to the people of Israel. When He sent out the Apostles on their first evangelistic mission, He ordered them, "Go not into the way of the Gentiles, and into any city of the Samaritans enter ye not; but go rather to the lost sheep of the house of Israel" (Matt. 10:5-6). This does not mean that He ignored individual Gentiles, because He did minister to a few (Matt. 8:5-13 and 15:21-28); but His major emphasis was on Israel.

After His resurrection, He commanded the Apostles to remain in Jerusalem and begin their ministry there (Luke 24:44-49). The period covered by Acts 1—7 is characterized by a ministry only to Jews or Jewish proselytes. It was not until Acts 8 that the Gospel went to the Samaritans; in Acts 10 it went to the Gentiles. Then, through the ministry of Paul, it went throughout the Roman Empire (Acts 13:1-3).

When He came and died, Jesus Christ confirmed the promises that God made to Abraham and the other "fathers" of the Jewish nation. (See Luke 1:30-33, 46-55, and 67-80.) Some of these promises have already been fulfilled, but many await fulfillment when He returns to earth to establish His Kingdom.

Was it selfish of God to emphasize the Jews? No, because through the Jews, He would send the Good News of salvation to the Gentiles. The first Christians were Jewish believers! "Salvation is of the Jews" (John 4:22). In the Old Testament period, God chose Israel to be a minister to the Gentiles; but instead, Israel copied the idolatrous ways of the Gentiles and had to be chastened. In the New Testament period, God chose Jewish believers to carry the Good News to the Gentiles, and they obeyed Him.

There is a beautiful progression in the promises that Paul quoted in verses 9 through 12.

- The Jews glorify God *among* the Gentiles (v. 9, quoting Ps. 18:49)
- The Gentiles rejoice *with* the Jews (v. 10, quoting Deut. 32:43)
- All the Jews and Gentiles *together* praise God (v. 11, quoting Ps. 117:1)
- Christ shall reign over Jews and Gentiles (v. 12, quoting Isa. 11:10)

Romans 15:8 covers the period of the Gospels and Acts 1—7. Romans 15:9 describes the ministry of Paul as he witnessed among the Gentiles. Romans 15:10 could be applied to the church council in Acts 15 when the Gentiles were given equal status "with his people." Today, Jews and Gentiles in the church are praising God together.

The word "trust" at the end of verse 12 is actually the word "hope." At one time the Gentiles were "without hope" (Eph. 2:12, NIV), but now in Christ they have hope. Not only do believers have hope, but they also have joy and peace and power (v. 13)! The Holy Spirit of God shares these blessings with them as they yield to Him.

Because the Jewish Christians were faithful to take the Gospel to the Gentiles, the nations of the world today have the opportunity to trust Christ as Saviour.

2. Paul's Ministry to the Gentiles (15:14-24)

Unless we understand the distinctive ministry of Paul, we will not fully appreciate the message of God's grace. Paul explained the characteristics of his ministry.

a. *It was received by grace* (15:14-15)—When he was Saul of Tarsus, the crusading rabbi, Paul knew nothing of the grace of God. He persecuted the Church and sought to destroy it. When Paul met Jesus Christ on the Damascus Road (Acts 9), he experienced the grace of God. It was God's grace that saved him, and it was God's grace that called him and made him an apostle (1 Cor. 15:8-11). "We have received grace and apostleship, for obedience to the faith among all nations, for His name" (Rom. 1:5). In Ephesians 3, Paul explained his ministry to the Gentiles in greater detail.

b. *It was centered in the Gospel* (15:16)—As mentioned before, Paul used two different words for *minister* in this verse, but the emphasis is on priestly service. Paul looked upon himself as a priest at the altar, offering up to God the Gentiles he had won to Christ. They were a "spiritual sacrifice" to the glory of God (see 1 Peter 2:5). Even his preaching of the Gospel was a "priestly duty" (NIV). This insight into ministry certainly adds dignity and responsibility to our service. It was important that the priests offer to God only that which was the best (see Mal. 1:6-14).

Note the involvement of the Trinity in the ministry of the Word. Paul was the minister of Jesus Christ; he preached "the Gospel of God"; and he served in the power of the Holy Spirit of God who sanctified his ministry. What a privilege, and yet what a responsibility, to be the servant of the Triune God, winning the lost to Jesus Christ! We must remember that soul-winning is a priestly ministry, a sacred obligation. And we must serve the Lord with dedication and devotion just as the priest in the temple.

c. *It was done for God's glory* (15:17)—"Therefore I glory in Christ Jesus in my service to God" (NIV). The word translated "glory" carries the idea of "boast, take pride in." Paul used it before in Romans 2:17, 23; 5:2-3, 11 ("joy"); 3:27, and 4:2. Paul was not bragging about his ministry. He was boasting in what the Lord had done. The apostle did not serve and suffer as he did just to make a name for himself, for he had a much higher purpose in mind. He wanted to bring glory to Jesus Christ. "That in all things He might have the preeminence" (Col. 1:18).

d. *It was done by God's power* (15:18-19)—The Holy Sprit empowered Paul to minister, and enabled him to perform mighty signs and wonders. The miracles God gave Paul to do were "signs" in that they came from God and revealed Him to others. And they were "wonders" in that they aroused the wonder of the people. But their purpose was always to open the way for the preaching of the Gospel. Miracles were given to authenticate the messenger and the message (Heb. 2:1-4). Miracles *by themselves* can never save the lost. When Paul healed the crippled man at Lystra (Acts 14), the immediate response was pagan: the people called Paul and Barnabas gods and tried to worship them! When Paul shared the Gospel with them, they did not respond so enthusiastically. Finally, the people stoned Paul and left him for dead outside the city walls.

The Spirit of God empowered Paul to share the Word, and the purpose was to "make the Gentiles obedient . . ." (Rom. 15:18). It was "by word and deed" that the apostle shared the Good News.

We may not be able to perform miracles today, since this was a special apostolic gift. But "by word and deed" we can share the love of God with the lost around us. Changes in conduct and character are just as much miracles of the Holy Spirit as the healing of the sick.

e. *It was according to God's plan* (15:20-24)— God had a special plan for Paul to follow: he was not to preach where any other apostle had ministered. (This is one evidence that Peter had not founded the churches at Rome, or had been to Rome; for this would have prevented Paul from going there.) "From Jerusalem and round about unto Illyricum" (v. 19) covers about 1,400 miles! When you consider the slowness of travel and the dangers involved (2 Cor. 11:26-27), you can appreciate the tremendous achievement of Paul's missionary ministry. While it is not wrong to enter into another man's labors (John 4:38), it is also good to have a pioneer ministry and take the Gospel to new territory. Paul cited Isaiah 52:15 as the divine approval for this kind of ministry.

The vast area of opportunity in other parts of the Empire kept Paul from visiting Rome sooner. He was not hindered from going to Rome by Satanic opposition or physical obstacles, but by the challenge of completing his work right where he was. He was so faithful in his evangelistic outreach that he was able to say that he had no more place to minister in those parts. This did not mean that Paul personally witnessed to every person in that area, but that he took the Gospel and left behind witnessing churches and Christians who would carry on the work. Paul finished one job before he

started another one, a good example for our evangelistic ministry today.

Paul's desire for many years had been to visit
Rome and then move on to Spain but there is no
record that he ever did. Tradition says that he did
go to Spain, and to Britain, after he was released,
but church tradition is not always to be trusted.

3. The Gentiles' Ministry to the Jews (15:25-33)

Paul and his associates had received a special offering from the Gentile churches in Greece for the
suffering Jewish saints in Jerusalem. Details about
this collection are recorded in 2 Corinthians 8 and
9. There were several purposes behind this special
offering. To begin with, it was an expression of love
on the part of the Gentiles toward their Jewish
brethren. Second, it meant practical relief at a time
when the poor Jewish believers needed it the most.
Third, it helped to unite Jews and Gentiles in the
church. It was a bond that brought them closer
together.

Paul looked upon this offering as the paying of
a debt. The Gentiles had received *spiritual* wealth
from the Jews. They now returned *material* wealth,
paying their debt. Paul considered himself a
"debtor" to the whole world (Rom. 1:14). He also
considered the Gentile Christians debtors to the
Jews, for it was the Jews who gave to the Gentiles
the Word of God and the Son of God. We Christians
ought to feel an obligation to Israel, and to pay
that debt by praying for Israel, sharing the Gospel,
and helping in a material way. Anti-Semitism has
no place in the life of a dedicated Christian.

Not only was this offering a payment of a debt,
but it was also "fruit" (Rom. 15:28). It was not
"loot" that Paul stole from the churches! It was

fruit—the natural result of their walk with the Lord
(see John 15:1-8).

When the life of the Spirit flows through a church,
giving is no problem. Paul, in 2 Corinthians 8:1-5,
described the miracle of grace that occurred in the
churches of Macedonia.

Paul was anxious that this offering be received
by the Jewish believers and be acceptable to them.
He wanted to bring about, under God, a closer
bond between the mother church at Jerusalem and
the daughter churches in other parts of the Empire.
Unfortunately, there were still Jews who opposed
the message of grace to the Gentiles and who
wanted the Gentiles to become Jews and accept
the Jewish Law. (Bible students call these people
"Judaizers." They followed Paul wherever he went
and tried to steal his churches from him. The Epistle
to the Galatians was written to combat their evil
works.)

The words "strive together" in verse 30 suggest
an athlete giving his best in the contest. Perhaps
the words "wrestling together" better express the
idea. This same term is used of the praying of
Epaphras in Colossians 4:12. This verse does not
mean that we must fight with God to get what we
need. Rather, it means our praying must not be a
casual experience that has no heart or earnestness.
We should put as much fervor into our praying as a
wrestler does into his wrestling!

4. The Believers' Ministry to Paul (16:1-27)

What a remarkable chapter! In it Paul greeted at
least 26 people by name, as well as two unnamed
saints; and he also greeted several churches that
were meeting in homes. He closed with greetings
from nine believers who were with him in Corinth

when he wrote the letter. What is the significance of this? It shows that Paul was a friend-maker as well as a soul-winner. He did not try to live an isolated life; he had friends in the Lord, and he appreciated them. They were a help to him personally and to his ministry. In my own reading of Christian biography, I have discovered that the servants whom God has used the most were people who could make friends. They multiplied themselves in the lives of their friends and associates in the ministry. While there may be a place for the secluded saint who lives alone with God, it is my conviction that most of us need each other. We are sheep, and sheep flock together.

a. *Some friends to greet* (16:1-16)—He began with Phebe, a member of the church at Cenchrea, and the lady who carried the letter to the saints at Rome. Never did a messenger carry a more important letter! Cenchrea was the seaport of Corinth, so Phebe was probably won to Christ during Paul's year and a half of ministry in Corinth. The word "servant" is the feminine of *deacon,* and some students believe she was a "deaconess" in the church. This is possible, because there were women in the Early Church who served by visiting the sick, assisting the young women, and helping the poor. Paul confessed that Phebe had been a helper (literally "protectress") of himself and other Christians. And he encouraged the church to care for her.

How we wish we had the details of the stories behind each of these names! We have met Priscilla and Aquila in the Book of Acts (18:1-3, 18-19, 26). Where and when they risked their lives for Paul, we do not know, but we are glad they did it! (See also 1 Cor. 16:19 and 2 Tim. 4:19.) At the time of this writing, they were in Rome and a church met in their house. In this chapter, Paul greeted a number of such assemblies (Rom. 16:10-11, 14-15).

Four persons are called "beloved" by Paul: Epenetus (v. 5), Amplias (v. 8), Stachys (v. 9), and Persis (v. 12). Paul would remember Epenetus in particular, for he was the first of his converts in Asia. Apparently he belonged to the household of Stephanas, for in 1 Corinthians 16:15 these people are also called "the firstfruits of Achaia!"

Andronicus and Junias are called "kinsmen," which may mean blood relatives of Paul, or only that they, too, were Jewish, possibly of the tribe of Benjamin like Paul. At one time they had been in prison with Paul. The word "apostle" here does not imply that they held the same office as Paul, but rather that they were "messengers" of the Lord. The word "apostle" has both a narrow and a broad meaning.

The Rufus mentioned in verse 13 may be the same as the one named in Mark 15:21, but we cannot be certain. If so, then Simon's experience at Calvary led to his conversion and that of his household. Paul and Rufus were not related. "His mother and mine" means only that Rufus' mother had been like a mother to Paul (see Mark 10:30).

This list shows the parts that people played in Paul's ministry and the ministry of the churches. Phebe was a "succourer" of many. Priscilla and Aquila were "helpers" and "laid down their own necks" for Paul. The conversion of Epenetus led to the salvation of others in Asia. Mary "bestowed much labor." Andronicus and Junias went to prison with Paul. One can only give thanks for these devoted saints who fulfilled their ministries to the glory of God. May we follow in their train!

b. *Some foes to avoid* (16:17-20)—Not everyone

was working with Paul for the spreading of the
Gospel. There were some who, for selfish reasons,
were dividing the churches by teaching false doctrine. These people were probably the same Judaizers who had given Paul trouble in other churches
(see Phil. 3:17-21). Instead of preaching the truth,
these men spread their own religious propaganda,
using deceit and clever speeches. We have the same
problem today, and Christians must beware of false
teachers. They come to your front door with maga-
zines, books, and tapes, trying to convince you that
they are teaching the truth. Paul gives two instructions: mark them (identify them), and avoid them.

It is a matter of obedience to the Lord and testimony to others. The issue is not making or keeping
friends, but pleasing the Lord and maintaining a
consistent testimony. Verse 20 suggests that these
false teachers really come from Satan, and one
day even he shall be completely defeated.

c. *Some faithful servants to honor* (16:21-24)—
What a roll call of heroes! Timothy was mentioned
often in the Book of Acts and the Epistles. He was
Paul's "son in the faith" and labored with Paul in
many difficult places. (See Phil. 2:19-24.) Lucius
was a fellow Jew, as were Jason and Sosipater. We
have no proof that this is the same Jason who pro-
tected Paul in Thessalonica (Acts 17:1-9). That
Jason was probably a Gentile.

Tertius was the secretary who wrote the letter
as Paul dictated it. Gaius was the man in whose
home Paul was residing at Corinth. First Corinthians 1:14 told how Paul won Gaius to Christ and
baptized him when he founded the church in Corinth. Apparently there was an assembly of believers
meeting in his house. Erastus held a high office in
the city, probably the treasurer. The Gospel

reached into high places in Corinth as well as into low places (1 Cor. 1:26-31; 6:9-11).

Verse 24 was probably written by Paul's own hand, since this was his "official seal" in every letter (see 2 Thes. 3:17-18).

The closing benediction is the longest one Paul ever wrote. It reflects his special ministry to the Gentiles. "The mystery" has to do with God's program of uniting believing Jews and Gentiles in the One Body, the Church (see Eph. 3). This was Paul's special message. It was because of this message that the Judaizers persecuted Paul, because they wanted to maintain Jewish privileges. Both Jews and Gentiles in the Roman churches needed to know what God's program was. Some of this Paul had explained in chapters 9 through 11.

Christians are established by the truth, which explains why Paul wrote this letter: to explain God's plan of salvation to Christians so they would be established, and so they would share the truth with the lost. After all, we cannot really share with others something we do not have ourselves.

This means that our own study of Romans should make us more stable in the faith, and more excited to share Christ with others. And the result: "To God only wise, be glory through Jesus Christ forever!"